2500
RANDOM
THINGS
ABOUT
ME
TOO

MATIAS VIEGENER

TrenchArt: Surplus

Les Figues Press
Los Angeles

2500 Random Things About Me Too ©2012 Matias Viegener
Introduction ©2012 Kevin Killian
Visual Art (back cover), Klaus Killisch, hippie guys (2), 2011,
collage on paper, 19.3 by 9.3 cm

2500 Random Things About Me Too
FIRST EDITION

Text design by Chris Hershey-Van Horn and Teresa Carmody

ISBN 13: 978-1-934254-35-6
ISBN 10: 1-934254-35-5
Library of Congress Control Number: 2012942151

Les Figues Press thanks its subscribers for their support and
readership. Les Figues Press is a 501(c)3 organization.
Donations are tax-deductible.

Les Figues would like to acknowledge the following individuals
for their generosity: Peter Binkow, Johanna Blakley, Lauren Bon,
Chris and Diane Calkins, Sarah de Heras, Pam Ore, Coco Owen,
Mary Swanson.

Les Figues Press titles are available through:
Les Figues Press, <http://www.lesfigues.com>
Small Press Distribution, <http://www.spdbooks.org>

Special thanks to Amanda Ackerman, Mario Macias, Courtney
Johnson, Erin Kilduff, Coco Owen, and Emma Williams.

TrenchArt 7/2

Book 3 of 6 in the TrenchArt Surplus

This project is supported in part
by a generous grant from the
National Endowment for the Arts.

ART WORKS.
arts.gov

Post Office Box 7736
Los Angeles, CA 90007
www.lesfigues.com

CONTENTS

INTRODUCTION

KEVIN KILLIAN

Facebook goes so fast that when Dodie told me Vanessa and Teresa were publishing Matias' Facebook "random thing" notes as a book, I frowned at my own blank mind. I couldn't remember them at first, then it came back, how day after day, I would encounter yet 25 more things Matias had written. When was that, literally or figuratively years ago? The problem with Facebook (!!!!—as if there were only one problem!) is that whatever one writes proceeds down the screen inexorably until it hits the point where it disappears from consciousness. Maybe you can retrieve it, I personally don't think so. Recently I wrote something on FB about Justin Bieber and Linda Norton commented, "So funny. (And that's saying something—this is the funniest thing you've said on FB since you posted that wisecrack about James Michener.)" It has been tormenting me for weeks now, wondering what I could possibly have said about James Michener that was so funny. I guess a normal man would just ask Linda Norton, but it's so shame-making! Matias' book addresses these questions and more. Really I could just write 1,000 words of introduction commenting, as Facebook has taught us to do, about every one of MV's observations. Yes, I too thought Patti Smith was cool. Peggy *is* a very cute dog. So you have Richard Burton's autograph? I have Elizabeth Taylor's. I watched the OJ Simpson car chase with Earl Jackson, Jr. But it behooves me to move beyond the particular, as you instantly will, into the realm of general knowledge this parataxis erects.

You can't put two words together without creating a meaning, and you can't make a list without inflecting narrative on your reader. Matias Viegener resists calling his book a memoir, but asks us to think of it as a "procedural experiment that comes to resemble and echo the memoir." That it does. I took advantage of the search engine and looked for my name in this book, found it more than once. I don't remember the incidents in question, but that doesn't mean they didn't happen; it just means their randominity hit an intense point—stabs and valleys in a cardiac flow chart. Viegener is on guard against the ways narrative never fails to take advantage of a mind momentarily at ease, and you'll find yourself constantly bumping your shins against these railings.

It isn't a memoir, but if it was, that would tie in with a long tradition of texts written by gay men in the form of fragments. You know how Muriel Rukeyser said that if one woman told the truth about her life, the world would split open? For gay men, the truth about our lives seems to resist taxonomy in some fundamental manner. Matias pointed to the charming, sometimes scary lists Joe Brainard compiled in his *I Remember* iterations; and to John Cage's attempts at autobiography. "It's like a combination of John Cage and Joe Brainard, writing yourself out in bits and pieces" (xxi 4). I thought also of Wittgenstein, of Cole Porter numbers like "Let's Do It" or "You're the Top," of *The White Paper* of Jean Cocteau—life told as erotic adventure, with everything else clipped away like a ransom note. I wonder if Susan Sontag pushed her famous "Notes on Camp" into numbered paragraphs as a sort of a rueful salute to the difficulty queers have often felt trying to convey the truth of their lives. Well, she would know, right?

Many men with smart phones, it is said nearly ninety percent of us, have used them to photograph their own hard-ons, but I expect it is mostly the gay men who have written out the list of every guy they've had sex with. Then there are lists that are nothing more than eliminations, as the one Matias plays to kill time. He tells us, in crowded places, of picking the person he'd most like to have sex with, then right down the line to the one he'd hate to have sex with (ix 20). Funny, I play that game in the opposite order (and maybe that's how I've lived my whole life). Elsewhere (xx 12) he observes astutely, "Making a list is not the same as writing about yourself. You have more defenses when you're talking about your problems and complaints. Like when you're telling a story."

In his essay "On Memory," Cocteau explains why he could write no autobiography. "In memory our rules no longer apply. Dead and living alike move together on an artificial stage under fatal lighting. The stage is free. It creates scenes, it builds up, it intermixes, it offers us shows far more truthful than realism, for that is merely a one-plane pandering to our limitations." Cocteau can go on and on like this, he's marvelous. "As we waken, supervision comes to life. Memory exposes its wares, but all it can offer are a few fragments, and those are given grudgingly."

I also commend to you Matias' attention to his pet, the aging, frail, nearly indomitable greyhound Peggy. Like another "not a memoir," J. R. Ackerley's *My Dog Tulip* (1956), we learn more about the man the more he tells us of his female counterpart, the bitch. Peggy weakens through the "real time" of the meme, perhaps during the actual time the numbers take to grow, to pass. "It's not as if she's becoming less and less of herself," observes her owner in li 7, "but certainly a lower calorie version of herself, with less frills." It's no coincidence that the book ends when the life of Peggy comes to an end, taken away by our narrator to be put down as gently and nebulously as the best of her life. When I was a boy in the New Narrative movement, one of our leaders defined literature as that which doesn't happen to animals; but in this lovely salute, for once the animal gets her due.

Kevin Killian
San Francisco, CA, 2012

2500
RANDOM
THINGS
ABOUT
ME
TOO

People think I'm American but inside I'm foreign.   1

German was my first language, and though I   2
learned English when I was five, I sometimes grope
for words. On the other hand, I can't find them in
German either. Then I'm stranded on a sand bank.

I don't want to tell people things they don't know   3
about me.

Once I wanted to tell all and confess everything   4
in colorful language and cracked metaphors, but
now that seems tiresome.

I suppose I could reveal trivial and partially true   5
things.

Yeah, I slept around.   6

Yeah, I took some drugs.   7

I was closer to my mother than my father.   8

My father is easier to get along with than my   9
mother though.

Uh, I have a lot of favorite books.   10

I hate when people ask me who my favorite writer is.   11

Or favorite artist.   12

I mean, what am I supposed to say? It's a sort of   13
mindless conversation topic. Like, what's your
favorite color?

14   Usually I just answer with what I suppose the person asking wants me to say.

15   No, I don't think it matters.

16   The best realization I ever had was that the universe is basically indifferent to us. It's neither for nor against us. And that indifference is a good thing, a really comforting thing. It's consistent, you can really say that about it.

17   I think conceptual art is great, but I hate when everyone says everything they do is conceptual. All they usually mean is that it has an idea in it. That's not conceptual art. Everything has an idea in it somewhere, even nothing.

18   Narrative is overrated. An addiction to transparency. A simple-minded need for linearity to organize a set of data. It doesn't have much to do with real life.

19   Of course I love a good story.

20   The best sex? The best sex I've ever had was with the worst boyfriend I ever had. Yup.

21   When I was a kid, the museum we went to most often was MOMA, the old MOMA, where *Guernica* hung on the landing by the top of the stairs. That was as close to church as we came. I remember looking at one of Ad Reinhardt's all-black paintings, and someone next to me said it was about "infinite absolute negativity." That was a formative moment for me.

22   Yes, punk rock, the 80s, the East Village. What I loved about punk then was how serious it was, and how realistic.

I really love people who sing out of tune. Morrissey,   23
Rufus Wainwright, Marlene Dietrich, Lotte Lenya.
Love them. I met Lotte Lenya once, when I was a
kid. My aunt was head of the Goethe-Institut in
NY, and she took me to lunch with her. We went
to Horn & Hardart, Lenya's favorite place to eat.
It was an automat, where you get your food pre-
made through little boxes with glass doors.

Borscht.   24

I've seen as many people destroyed by success as   25
by failure. You don't get much empathy when
success overwhelms you. Nor with failure. No
one wants to talk about you then either. "The
thing about American success," said Gertrude
Stein, "is American failure."

ii

Ja, Gesamtkunstwerk.   1

I do believe in genius. I've met at least one: Kathy   2
Acker.

This is pretty unbearable, isn't it?   3

I'll make more of an effort.   4

I went to Buenos Aires, where I was born, for the   5
first time in 32 years and the most familiar thing
about it was how it smelled.

For many years when I was very anxious I would   6
close my eyes and visualize this small green shovel
my mother had. I would think about what it was
for, just digging in the soil. And then I could calm
down, because it meant everything and nothing.

My favorite things to visit are probably hot springs.   7
Real ones, built into cliffs, or mud holes in the

desert. They're like the hot womb of the earth, taking us back despite our feckless ways.

8   I'm trying to be sincere now.

9   When I read up to numbers 6 and 7, I guess the message is that I'm earthy.

10   Or the message could be I want you to think I'm earthy.

11   Maybe by expressing my cynicism just now I am forestalling your critical reaction and demonstrating my ineluctable earthiness and sincerity. Like an apotropaic expression.

12   I love big words, but mostly I avoid using them because I don't want to sound pedantic. Why use a long word when a short one will do?

13   I don't like candy.

14   My dog Peggy is almost 14 and pretty deaf. She can't see that well and has arthritis.

15   I think she has some kind of Alzheimer's too because sometimes she walks around with a dazed expression, and she looks up at me as if asking who are you, or where am I, or how did I get here? Somehow this isn't sad to me though. It feels like the natural course of things.

16   I've been writing a piece about me and Peggy for a long time. It's about interspecies relationships.

17   You could say I'm interested in other forms of language, how we communicate with each other. Also how others communicate with us, especially the others who can't talk.

18   I have trouble finishing things, but not starting them.

Overall I believe women are better people than men.   19

I am attracted to people who are verbal and articulate.   20

Almost everyone I've been involved with is taller than me, and I wonder what this says about me.   21

I guess I should tell another heartwarming story.   22

One of the worst things about writing is the general expectation that what you say has to make sense.   23

Nonsense.   24

Have you noticed that it's not cool right now to act like you have no financial problems?   25

iii

I remember reading Joe Brainard for the first time and how I wasn't taken by *I Remember* at all, until I got about a third of the way through. Memories are cumulative and Brainard's book proves the futility of linear narrative in relation to the past. Each entry thickens and complicates Brainard's life or his "identity." At the end there's a kind of cloud of Joe, a mass of being there or having been there.   1

Sometimes I hate David Burns. Sometimes I love him. Often I like him a lot. Other times I have no opinion.   2

I remember thinking I would never write my own *I Remember*. What would be the point?   3

On some level I also don't actually remember much, and much of what I do remember is what people tell me to remember.   4

5 Every week or two I wake up thinking of my mother and crying. Somehow it makes me feel better. I don't think this will ever stop.

6 My cousins live all over the world and often I don't get to see their houses at all, but when I do I've always been struck by some kind of familiarity in them. There are always dried flowers, rocks, a few kinds of art, but no posters; and something primitive, a basket or an old thing whose most vivid characteristic is peeling or cracked paint.

7 Does that last one count as a heartwarming story?

8 My worrying about money has no particular relation to how much money I have or how things look. It must be hormonal or something.

9 For the most part I do not believe in genius.

10 When I flew over the Amazon (from Panama to Buenos Aires), I got an intense and haunting sensation of some green, witchy power calling me from below, something really wide and fertile to the point of rotting and coming back to life; moaning, dying, and coming back to life again.

11 Of course I have no particular relation to the Amazon except that it—and I guess the Gulf of Mexico—was on the trajectory of my family's first flight to the US.

12 That's not heartwarming at all.

13 But it is a selective set of facts. I could also count all the states between, say, Florida and NY, and all the non-jungle areas of Argentina up to the Amazon.

14 I kind of hate how random things you don't know about someone eventually always land on immigration.

It's very hard to talk about immigration or dogs   15
without sentimentality.

I remember when I thought *Einstein on the Beach*   16
was the most brilliant thing I'd ever seen, and then
later when I thought it was kind of embarrassing
and kitschy.

"I was in this prematurely air-conditioned   17
supermarket and there were all these aisles and
there were bathing caps you could buy that had
these kind of Fourth of July plumes on them
that were red and yellow and blue and I wasn't
tempted to buy one but I was reminded of the
fact that I had been avoiding the beach."

I got separated from my friend Vicki when I saw   18
Einstein on the Beach and had to sit alone. The
handsome guy next to me started to press his
thigh against mine and then touched my legs and
after many hours he touched my hand and we
held hands. We got to groping each other, and
when it was over I had to go back to my friend
Vicki, but later that night I went to his hotel
room. He was French, his name was Christian,
and we had great sex. He had to go back to Paris
the next day. He started to call me and send letters
(it was before email), and then I went to visit him
for a week in Paris and everything fell apart. On
the last night, we had such a big fight I called
my cousin Irene, who lived nearby, to stay at her
house, but finally he begged me to stay the last
night with him. After that we never talked again.

Oh, that night at *Einstein on the Beach* he wore   19
a wedding ring, which he took off at some point
trying to get me not to notice it. He wasn't
married, but he told me later he wore it so straight
women wouldn't make passes at him.

20 I'm not sure if there is any connection between him and Einstein except the obvious. Or between me and him, except Einstein and the obvious.

21 21 is a number I like.

22 My father was a jewelry designer.

23 Christian was the director of a big contemporary dance company.   That was when I thought dance, and theater for that matter, were really relevant and important. As time went on those things seemed less interesting until, with some exceptions, I couldn't much stand them.

24 You'll notice no one in my family wears jewelry. No one really likes it.

25 A psychic once told me I needed to have some metal near my body, and later I got a watch with a steel watchband. Ever since then I'm never without a watch with a steel watchband.

iv

1 In my dream last night I lifted a patch of my hair and underneath was all gray and silver.

2 I used to worry that, as a writer, I wasn't experimental enough.

3 My mother hated her salt and pepper hair and always wanted her hair to be silver. A mop of silver hair, and she got it. She dreaded the thought of being a vegetable when she got old, and she didn't get that. She died of a cerebral hemorrhage, out like a light bulb.

4 Long ago I tried to write poems by taking out all the conjunctions and adjectives. It didn't work.

For a while I was a performance artist. I didn't 5
really like being in front of an audience though.

I tend to use the same password all the time, 6
which is a combo of an old pet's name and a
childhood address. In this world of little internet
security, it is not, as they say, very robust of me.

That feels like a very intimate statement. 7

People are going to start having ideas about me if 8
they keep reading this.

I love movies that make me cry. I loved *Beaches*. 9

I need to make this really boring and pedantic to 10
drive people away.

Also, I should cut out all the parts with sex or 11
with family stories. People really love that stuff.

I lived right on the beach for almost three years 12
and I think it changed my DNA. The house was
on the last row before the sand, and you had to
go down a steep hill about 250 feet, and for every
foot I think my tension dropped one percent.

Sometimes I dream about that house at the 13
beach. I lived with my boyfriend, Mike Kelly, in
the guesthouse above the garage and the landlady
never knew I lived there. We never locked the
door, so everyone would just walk in. Sometimes,
to throw her off guard, I'd ask where Mike Kelly
was, or tell her to tell him I'd dropped by.

Yes, she drank a lot. 14

Once there was an earthquake in the middle of 15
the night and we all ran outside. She was so upset,
she didn't notice I was there.

16   She is dead now and the house is torn down. There's a McMansion in its place.

17   The house was in Manhattan Beach, 3000 miles from Manhattan, NY.

18   I don't like how this is starting to get narrative.

19   Conceptual art generally has a specific formulation that is iterated through some kind of repetition in the work or in the execution itself.

20   No, I don't intend to repeat anything here.

21   I have a tattoo on my right leg; it says "something."

22   This is truly a random detail about me, because I got it randomly.

23   I always wanted a tattoo but I could never decide what it should be. A few years ago Shelley Jackson asked for volunteers to have the words of her story "Skin" tattooed on them. You signed up and got sent a word and that was it, except I think you got one more chance if you didn't like the word you drew. We got to pick where the word would be, and no one but us knows the whole text of the story. We're her words.

24   What I liked about "something" is that I didn't have to choose it.

25   Also that when someone asks me what's that on my leg, I can say "something."

v

1   After my high school graduation, we went to the restaurant on top of the World Trade Center.

I prefer dark chocolate to milk chocolate. In fact, it can hardly be too dark. When it's good it's like eating dirt. Kind of like beets. 2

In 1976 we painted the fire hydrant in front of our house red, white, and blue. A few people did it, but then word got around that it was illegal, and they had to stay black and silver. Actually, I think we painted it after we knew we weren't supposed to. It's about the only patriotic thing I can remember from my childhood. 3

About two years ago I visited that house for the first time in about 20 years. The hydrant was chipped and faded and still red, white, and blue. 4

Oh, I came to America on a propeller plane. I love that fact! 5

Also, I think we took the Brooklyn Ferry on our way from the airport when we arrived. 6

All these facts make me feel so historical. You don't get to feel history until a certain point in your life. I guess 9/11 made a lot of people feel historical. 7

I read about Patti Smith in the *Village Voice* when I was a teenager and bought her album, and I was the only person I knew who loved her. I remember listening at home to the line "I haven't fucked much with the past, but I've fucked plenty with the future." My parents were there but they didn't say anything, and to this day I wonder if they didn't care what she said or if they didn't hear it. 8

Maybe I should talk about that. 9

Did I fuck with the future? 10

I can certainly say my life is nothing like what I imagined it might be like then. 11

12   Christine Wertheim and I often talk about then and now, what we then thought we'd be now. I didn't really have a plan though. I do remember I intensely did not want to be bored. I wanted to be interested by my own life.

13   So, based on the above criteria, I've succeeded.

14   I didn't really want to do this list, but after I got tagged by a few people I like, I got tagged by a cute guy I don't really know. So at first I did it to get him to notice me.

15   He hasn't said anything and besides it's too much work for someone you don't know, so now it's sort of something I do because I started it, and I don't want to seem like a quitter.

16   Now I really hope he doesn't read this.

17   A man I know claimed that Roland Barthes was holding his dissertation when he got run over by a truck.

18   Christine Wertheim got assigned the words "away [comma]" for her tattoo, and she doesn't really like them. She wanted my word, "something," but I wouldn't trade for it. I liked "away [comma]" well enough, but I wanted to be assigned my tattoo, not to choose it.

19   I don't buy it.

20   My parents hated flags. In fact they hated all signs of nationalism.

21   Everybody has random details about themselves.

22   I think many stories are stories by virtue of our wanting to make random details into narratives.

Christine still doesn't like "away [comma]" and 23
hasn't gotten her tattoo. She says it's like we are a
box, and on my box it says "something" and on
hers it says "away." My box has something, but
her contents are away.

Narrative is something created by the reader's 24
need.

But the worst kind of narratives are those wrested 25
into place by pushy or needy writers.

vi

I had a boyfriend who was a prostitute. 1

Actually, he became a prostitute. He wasn't one 2
for the first two years. When we broke up, he
accused me of being something like a racist.

My parents did not fuck much with the past or 3
the future. Mostly the world fucked with them.

He said breaking up with someone because he was 4
a prostitute was like breaking up with someone
because he was black.

He needed the money to complete an expensive 5
art project.

The best thing I discovered in Hawaii was the 6
little fish. I'd been snorkeling before but suddenly
I was surrounded by colorful little fish and coral,
and it felt as close as possible to traveling to
another planet.

The fish are just present unto themselves, no 7
plans, no regrets, just the moment.

The thing I like least about teaching is faculty 8
meetings.

9   I'm always happy when I am naked.

10   Silver Lake reminds me of San Francisco. It's hilly and green.

11   Another thing I dislike about teaching is committees, which lead invariably to more meetings.

12   I do like search committees though. It's the only real power you have, choosing who else you get to work with.

13   When I told my mother that I was unhappy because my ex was working as a prostitute, she wasn't shocked at all.

14   Prostitution is necessary, she said. But you wouldn't want your lover to be a prostitute.

15   When I look back, this is one of the reasons I think my mother was a remarkable human.

16   There's something unsettling to me about the presence of Mac Geniuses, having to wait for them to talk to you, them having all the answers.

17   My mother keeps returning into my lists.

18   You never escape your mother, which is especially poignant when your mother is dead and she has fully and entirely escaped you. If she wasn't the end referent to most things before that, she is after.

19   I had a boss who was also a psychoanalyst, and her secretary, Lois, once told me she would often ask if Lois thought one or another of us was narcissistic or Oedipal, etc.

20   I think Dennis Cooper is one of the great living writers.

I wanted to say more about the boyfriend who was a prostitute, but most of my impulses are to talk about my mother. 21

I guess he was necessary, and the awfulness of it too. 22

Yes, it took a long time to feel right again. 23

He owed me some money and for a long time I nagged him to pay me back. 24

It was symbolic: to get back the money he was getting from other men for what I once got for nothing. 25

vii

I am running out of random things and it's a struggle not to turn away from randomness toward stories, strategies, lies, bluffs, extended anecdotes, etc. 1

A common topic of dinner conversation in my family was suicide, especially in relation to being old and wanting to die with dignity. 2

The Holocaust, or the War, was another topic, and it was more tense. 3

These two topics were not overtly related. 4

Wow, when I was a kid "the War" [*der Krieg*] could only mean one thing. 5

In high school I met the Fonz from *Happy Days* and the mayor of NY in Gracie Mansion. They collected a handful of smart kids from each school and sent us off on these missions. 6

7 We also met Tennessee Williams, who seemed kind of drunk, who talked to the nearly three hundred of us in a small theater, and who was the first really successful or famous gay person I saw. But it was clear he was not happy.

8 I love the way my dog smells, especially her paws. My mother also liked the smell of her dog's paws.

9 Growing up in New York meant knowing Italians, Jews, Irish Catholics, African-Americans, Chinese, and Puerto Ricans. Sort of in that proportion.

10 Peggy in fact smells more as she gets old, has bad breath, and everything else.

11 I hardly knew any real WASPS until I went to college. Actually I only really met them when I went to graduate school.

12 Now I know more WASPS than ever before.

13 For a long time I was fixated on Virginia Woolf. I could not stop reading her and everything I wrote sounded like her; I could not write more than twenty words without a semicolon.

14 Virginia Woolf is a master of the semi-colon.

15 Her work is so refractive and so deeply inside what it is to be present, or conscious—at least in one version of what it is to be conscious, or to be in time—it's probably a nostalgic version for us.

16 I'm having a hard time today.

17 I love going to the gym.

18 I am actually a shy person. Now that's a classic random list thing to say.

I was shy but I'm not any more. At a certain point it was too much work or too hard to manage. 19

The key to a successful garden is to work off the color green. People try to avoid it but it's the basic ground, except in arid climates where it is grey or beige. 20

I just got asked for a list of fifteen albums that had such a profound effect they changed my life. No! This is too much. It's too invasive. I'm not doing it. 21

I once had a date with a guy who boasted that he had eaten oatmeal for breakfast for the last ten years, as if that was an achievement of some kind. 22

In the garden I like to play grey tones against reddish or purple ones. 23

The only thing I won't write here is "I have nothing to say." 24

I can't go to the gym today. 25

viii

Piss, shit, and vomit do not gross me out. Blood is a little harder. 1

The main thing wrong with my father's wife is that she isn't my mother. It makes me feel guilty to write that. 2

She's a great person otherwise. 3

The more I do these lists, the less I believe in randomness. Everything is part of a calculation of some kind. 4

There are no accidents. 5

6   Wait! I think there are. Really.

7   I had an accident last fall and totaled my car. But it was my fault. I was looking at my new iPhone, two blocks from my house, because you can check the traffic on the route you're about to take.

8   You need to hold on to the idea that accidents are possible. And that they have no purpose, so that you, we, or I can spend time making sense of them and filling them with meaning.

9   I think Dodie Bellamy and Kevin Killian are the Virginia and Leonard Woolf of our time, only Kevin writes better than Leonard.

10   Actually, Vanessa Place and Teresa Carmody are the Virginia and Leonard Woolf of our time, because of their press (and better writing than Leonard's).

11   It's hard to know in what tense to speak of my parents. My mother is dead and my father is alive.

12   Well, maybe Vanessa and Teresa are more like Gertrude Stein and Alice Toklas, for obvious reasons. But this ill fits them as well.

13   The first graffiti I remember contemplating was on City Hall when I was 14. It was "Faggots unite against patriarchy."

14   Some things I've strived to cut out of my writing: family, identity, lovable animals, references to other books or artists, being gay, using fragments, and trying too hard to unify parts.

15   Earlier, when I was thinking about WASPS and then about Virginia Woolf, it did not occur to me that of course Virginia Woolf is a real WASP.

Airports depress me. I don't associate them with vacations or travel, but with rupture, immigration, and never seeing people again. 16

My resistance to telling anyone what music I like is very strong. It just seems much too personal to me. 17

And then some people, like David Burns, suggest I don't really have a relationship to music. 18

Often I get up about halfway through the night to eat a banana. 19

Hasn't everybody who is trapped in a long line, like at the post office, played that game where you have to pick who you'd have sex with first, if you had to, one by one, down to the person you'd least want to have sex with? 20

Telling people what music I like feels too vulnerable. 21

I bite my nails. 22

I have found that you are judged more by the music you listen to than what you wear, how you look, or what books you like. 23

I stop biting my nails for months at a time but it always starts up again. 24

It's tempting to end every list with something that seems conclusive or that ties up something I said earlier. 25

ix

I'm going to try to be more upbeat today, less melancholic and sentimental. 1

2   Earlier today I ate what you could call a perfect, resonant grapefruit.

3   There are certain stretches of freeway whose architecture and general swoop or swerve take my breath away.

4   My father and his wife have two parrots, a mean one from the Yucatan named Oscar and an African Grey named Kivu. They talk a lot. My father doesn't really like them but hasn't said so to his wife.

5   My analyst once said that my nail biting was a symptom of my fear of my own aggression. If I let my nails grow I think they will be so big that I could rip someone's head off with a slap.

6   The parrots mostly say Hello, and each other's names and bird-related things; at some point they got taught a lot of predictable things like the theme song for the *Bridge Over the River Kwai*, which they now whistle off-key. They can't keep a pitch.

7   I was in a relationship with someone for over two years, and over that time he said many crazy things to me about me. He was insecure and probably immature and I decided that I would ignore those things because I knew better.

8   When we broke up, wouldn't you know that every one of those crazy things he said came back to roost in my head?

9   From this I learned that it is very important not to let people say crazy things about you to you for very long. In the end, we hear everything, even when we think we're ignoring it.

10   My mother collected old moonshine jugs and salt pottery from New England. She had dozens of pieces.

For the last few years I've been sleeping in the bed of my guest room rather than my own bed. I like it better.   11

Two weeks ago I ate one of the best cheeses I've had in a long time. It was an Italian soft goat cheese wrapped in chestnut leaves. It tasted really leafy-earthy and nutty.   12

I once read that cheeses wrapped in leaves or straw can't be imported to the US, and ever since then I look for them everywhere.   13

There are a lot of them and my theory is there used to be many more, since leaves were the first wrapping material.   14

I love beets.   15

I like to have at least a hundred dollars in cash in my wallet.   16

When I was young, I also met Edward Albee and Allen Ginsberg, not at the same time though. I talked to Allen but not to Edward, who did not seem like anyone you'd want to talk to.   17

I saw Borges read once, at the MLA in NY. He was very old and blind, and someone had to lead him to the podium. I can't remember what he read or if he read from memory, but I remember his voice.   18

I wonder what it would be like to go through these lists and black out all proper names and even all nouns.   19

My father's wife is losing her memory, but she can play the flute perfectly. She's played all her life. Probably music skills are lodged in a different part of the brain.   20

21   My uncle George, who is also my father's wife's father (a long story), was a concert pianist, and he lost all his memory by the time he was 80; the last thing to go was his piano playing.

22   I remember once we found George in our garden and he didn't know who he was or why he was there.

23   I did set out to write happy things, but this isn't really an unhappy memory, just one memory among others.

24   I am tired of using I, me, my, and mine here.

25   The rain in Spain stays mainly on the plain.

x

1   It can work better in a mess than in a clean, empty workspace.

2   The concise, careful, and expressive use of language always impresses it.

3   It just lost a list of random things; the list got accidentally deleted.

4   It's kind of glad.

5   Even though it once took great delight in growing marijuana, it doesn't really like pot very much. It loves a horticultural challenge.

6   Once it had sex with a guy who was a Cher fetishist. When it arrived, all the lights were off, but later the guy turned the lights on and suddenly the room was filled with Cher memorabilia. First it thought things would be ok, but soon it had to leave.

One of the things it really hates is when writers   7
can only explain their work or explain how to
write in terms of intuition. For example: the story
just finds its own shape, or: just let your character
tell you what s/he wants.

On the other hand, if you accept, as it has, that   8
there is no such thing as randomness really, then
intuition comes to mind as the driving force
behind any random list.

For a few days it started to keep a back-up list   9
to feed its list when it ran out of random things.
But the back-up ran out quickly and now it sits
torturing itself for entries sometimes.

Today one of the parrots made a gurgling sound   10
like running water, and it began to think about
what parrots did before people, and of course all
they had to imitate were natural sounds.

The gurgling of water is one of the nicest sounds   11
on earth.

Many non-human sounds are nice, and almost all   12
nasty sounds come from humans somehow.

Oscar the parrot will take a chunk out of you if   13
you don't pay attention.

You cannot turn yourself into an it, even when   14
you want to. You are not it. You're never it.

Kivu, the other parrot, was raised by my father's   15
wife, and you can pet him and he will take little
loving nips at your fingers.

He is an African Grey, just like Alex, the famous   16
parrot with the largest vocabulary of any bird
ever. Alex died recently and there's a really awful
book by his owner about his life story. I guess

it's no surprise, but the book is really all about his owner.

17   The parrots also make intriguing mechanical sounds like a phone ringing or a knock on the door.

18   I'm trying to come up with something sexy or illicit to spark people's attention.

19   There's a whole sappy thing about parrots and language and feelings and intelligence.

20   No one wants to feel alone.

21   The African Grey makes a clicking sound with his beak and tongue, as do certain tribes in the Congo. No one knows if one is imitating the other. It's a source of some speculation.

22   Sometimes I think of more things after I've finished a list than when I am working on one.

23   When I was a kid, we'd sing the following tune to the song from the *Bridge Over the River Kwai*:

24   Comet, it makes your mouth turn green / Comet tastes just like gasoline / Comet will make you vomit / So take some Comet, and vomit, today!

25   I've never been in the hospital.

xi

 1   Baby talk fascinates me, and I am attracted and repulsed by it in equal measure.

2   My parents never spoke to us in baby talk. They thought of it as a very American thing.

For many years my mother's aunt would come to visit us every summer from Germany, and she talked baby talk to me and my brother, even though my mother forbade her to do so. In retrospect, I think they were embarrassed about her because she was such an ordinary person. She was like the main character in Flaubert's "Un Coeur Simple." 3

Something about my great aunt's baby talk would make me dizzy with pleasure, slightly sickened and exhilarated. 4

When I look back on it now, I see in this the close link between the abject and the cute. 5

I talk to myself, hum, and make emphatic sounds (ugh, err, hmm, etc.) more than ever before. If I live long enough, I will end up like a Kurt Schwitters sound-machine piece. 6

The parrots groom each other all the time. Oscar is somewhere between 50 and 75 years old. No one knows. Kivu is 14, a teenager. Actually, he only gets groomed and doesn't groom Oscar. 7

A lot of old age is about keeping warm, making food, and finishing your tasks. 8

My first pet was a white cat we found on vacation in Vermont. My brother and I named her Fluffy. She was mean and never let you touch her. 9

Then we had a series of other cats, mostly all tabby cats. They were all incredibly sweet, but each one lived no more than two years. One after another they got sick, got run over, or just disappeared. 10

Fluffy lived for about twenty years. Even after college, I'd come home and there she'd be, hissing at me. From this I deduced that the good die young, and the mean ones live as long as they want. 11

12   When the cats disappeared or our goldfish died, my mother never said anything until we asked, and then we had to press her to tell us the truth. Later she said she wanted to shelter us from death.

13   I think the deaths in my life, including my mother's death, would have been easier for me if I understood death earlier and more often.

14   Sofas have been a source of comfort to me.

15   My father and his wife's sofa is sort of beige striped with some woven floral design. It makes me think of other sofas.

16   When I was a kid, we had a kind of plush, beige sofa that I started to dislike when one of my friends said it didn't match the carpet or the chairs. He was gay. That sofa went from comforting me to embarrassing me.

17   Nina, my father's wife, is losing her memory.

18   Later we had a leather sofa that was cool because no one else had one.

19   We had a long talk today, my father, Nina, her daughter, and I, about provisions for the future. At least now we all talk about what's happening, but it's still hard to get specific about things like nursing homes.

20   Last year Nina asked us to remind her when she forgot things, which we did; but now she forgets many things and if we reminded her, we'd talk about it too much.

21   My cousin Bettina, who is a doctor, is here too. She got sick last night with this flu that everybody in Charlottesville has had. You throw up all night, then you have diarrhea, then you're weak for days.

I think antidepressants are mostly a good thing. 22

Nina doesn't remember much of our conversation 23
any more, and my father missed big chunks
because his hearing is bad.

When I look at Bettina, sometimes I see a straight 24
female version of who I might have been. I'm
closer to her than my brother. When I was little,
I wanted to marry her.

I'm waiting to see if I get the flu too. 25

xii

I had sex in an airplane once. It was a very late 1
flight from NY to LA, nearly empty (you can tell
this is long ago). He sat alone in the aisle opposite
mine, and after looking at each other a lot, we
ended up in the bathroom together.

Afterward we pretended nothing happened. 2

My boyfriend at the time picked me up at the 3
airport.

I slept so hard on the plane after I had sex that, 4
even if I had been inclined to feel guilty, it seemed
like a lot of time had passed.

Not far from where my father lives is Monticello, 5
the house of Thomas Jefferson, which is a real
study in America and the Enlightenment.

My favorite thing about Monticello is the tunnel 6
under the entire house where they carried the
food in and the chamber pots out.

All the people who did the work in Monticello 7
were Thomas Jefferson's slaves.

8   There is very little in Monticello about Sally Hemings, the slave with whom Jefferson had several children.

9   Jefferson's bed is in the main part of the house, on the first floor, and it is between two rooms, open to each side, which kind of makes it the eye of the house.

10   I think the phrase "to have" sex is odd.

11   Airplanes seem to bottle up my thinking. It's not just the air that is pressurized.

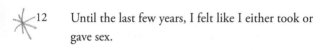

12   Until the last few years, I felt like I either took or gave sex.

13   I'm relieved to be older and less marketable.

14   For a long time I cried every time I took off from NY.

15   You don't realize how much NY is about fame and success until you live somewhere else. Except of course the same thing is true of LA.

16   After you take off, you seem to leave your emotions behind.

17   After your thirties, ambition to succeed takes the place of lust.

18   My father's wife, Nina, is not just losing her memory but also her sense of balance. She keeps tripping, and since nothing is wrong with her feet, the doctors now say it's her motor coordination.

19   Nina's grandparents died in Auschwitz and Theresienstadt.

My father and Nina knew each other as children, but Nina's family left Germany in 1936. 20

Our families have known each other for four generations. 21

Nina grew up in refugee housing in NY. She went to Barnard and was an Italian professor at the University of Illinois. She was a Dante scholar. 22

For many years Nina would not speak German. She speaks more now, because my father often lapses between German and English, especially when he talks to her. 23

I seem to have given up avoiding narrative. 24

They talk about the War a lot. 25

xiii

The only concentration camp I've been to is Sachsenhausen. It's near Berlin and a lot of homosexuals were imprisoned there. 1

When I was a kid, it was not good to be German. The Germans were still the most evil people in the world. 2

I remember once my mother told me we weren't German, we were European. 3

I grew up in a very Jewish neighborhood, but no one considered us Jewish, and neither did we think of ourselves as Jewish. 4

I just got two emotional emails from Mark So. It seems my random things have been stirring him up. 5

Some of them stir me up too, and others leave me numb. 6

7   Sometimes nothing comes, so I force it. There's nothing random about that.

8   My brother and I were sent to Sunday School at a Lutheran church.

9   Nina's mother, Hilde, was my brother's godmother. She was a zealous converted Catholic, and she insisted that even if my parents had no religion, we should have a choice.

10 The Catholic church was far and Our Savior Lutheran was a block away, so my brother and I went there for two years until we decided we didn't like it any more.

11 My parents were not happy when we came home and told them they wouldn't go to heaven if they didn't come to church with us.

12 I can't really abide any great religiosity in a person. Except maybe a silent one.

13 A place that made a big impression on me that I can hardly remember now is Mont St. Michel.

14 What is a single random thing? One fact? A complete sentence? Sometimes a random fact needs to be rounded out.

15 Some random facts only make sense when set in relation to each other.

16 Another sofa that helped me a great deal in life was Kaucyila Brooke's down-stuffed, red damask sofa, on which I spent almost two weeks. I had just had a bad breakup, and I did not want to be in my own house alone.

17 I was the first person to put incandescent lights into an office at CalArts; the fluorescent

lights made me crazy. Now most people have incandescent lights.

It is hard to say anything new about a concentration camp. 18

How could it happen? 19

How, in Europe? 20

One of the films I hate the most is *Life is Beautiful*. 21
I don't know what's more awful, the concentration camp or Roberto Benigni's character. Treacle from start to finish.

Sachsenhausen and Auschwitz prove that nothing 22
is really random, and that actually many things may be part of an evil plan.

When grapefruits are in season, I tend to eat one 23
every day.

I teach a class on pornography in which we do 24
not look at any images, only pornographic texts.

Treacle is one of my favorite words. 25

xiv

My favorite part of a man's body is his neck. 1

I overheard my father and Nina talking about 2
being old. Nina had seen a photo of them, and she asked my father if they were really so crooked. She said she didn't feel so hunched over.

My father said they were hunched over, and that 3
he didn't feel crooked inside either. But yes, they were old.

4   I dread the idea that this is turning into some kind of memoir.

5   My analyst once suggested that what I was looking for in men was their American quality.

6   There is something so nice about a list.

7   The middle class is the only class that hates itself. The working class doesn't, the rich don't. I think it's that self-hatred that makes so many artists ultimately come out of the middle class.

8   There was a kind of belief in my family that many or even most people eat the wrong way, read the wrong things, and think the wrong thoughts. But you weren't supposed to spend a lot of time criticizing them.

9   But then there was also a distrust of what you call "the elite."

10   David Burns accuses me of hating rich people.

11   There's a very German way of being both bohemian and bourgeois at the same time.

12   Something I noticed about the Language Poets is how they got trapped in their own apparatus. They kind of built this fast race car and then turned it into a hearse.

13   My mother grew up Catholic, and she was dragged from funeral to funeral of people she barely knew. She hated the Catholic church. But once, when she was in the hospital for surgery, my father and I were surprised to find she checked the box for last rites on her admission papers.

14   Between that and her death was nearly twenty years, but she did not have last rites when she died.

What I loved about the Language poets was   15
their use of parataxis: the list, the pieces strung
together one by one, nothing but proximity or
semiotics to connect them.

How is it that a person's family gets to echo   16
around in their head for so long?

I guess because they got there first.   17

My father's sister did have last rites, and he used   18
to joke about how a handsome Jesuit priest got to
her. Jesuits are sophisticated, and they beguiled
her with clever stories.

There was a running joke in my family based on   19
something my mother once said on a trip in the
Adirondacks: *das könnte in Europa sein.* So for a
long time anything that was special or nice "could
be in Europe." A nice painting, a forest, or a good
yogurt.

I like men's hands too, and their arms.   20
Appendages, I guess, is what I like.

Europa. This thing on my neck.   21

Maybe that isn't it. Maybe it's just too hard to be   22
present with anything, so you liken it to something
else. Maybe everybody picks something else to
absorb them.

Europa. It sounds so melodramatic. Some group   23
of people's dreams about something.

I remember once a man admiring our garden   24
upstate; he asked my mother if she had learned to
garden in the old country.

No, she said. From books. We learned to garden   25
from books.

xv

1   I tortured my brother with a bottle of milk. Holding it slowly over the kitchen floor as I poured it out, I'd call my mother and say he had spilled the milk again. He would stand there paralyzed, screaming that it wasn't him.

2   My mother caught on eventually.

3   I am vexed by Kenny Goldsmith, who says, "If it doesn't exist on the internet, it doesn't exist."

4   What does he mean by exist?

5   It has always bothered me that we have such a prejudice for things that exist over things that don't exist. It's a failure of ambition. It means we can't imagine anything that isn't already there.

6   A thing that doesn't exist is not nothing. It might be something we don't yet know exists.

7   I wish I could remember some more famous people I've met. I think they're good on this list because they give people something to latch on to.

8   After my father got his first computer at age 73, I asked him if it was the biggest technological change he'd ever witnessed.

9   He said the biggest technological change for him was the telephone, because then you could talk to people who weren't there.

10   I remember discovering Marxism for the second time. The first time was in high school, and I thought it was the coolest word ending in -ism, so I wrote a big paper on it.

My father grew up in the country and saw the arrival of electricity, radio, and the telephone in his childhood. — 11

Even in the liberal 70s, something about Marxism seemed radical to me. — 12

Then in college and grad school, I was swept away by words and language and philosophy. — 13

First I thought structuralism and then post-structuralism could explain everything. — 14

The second time I discovered Marxism is when I read *The Prison House of Language,* and suddenly I was sprung. — 15

You're assuming it's the same me each time I write a line here. — 16

OK, no. I'm assuming you're assuming, and of course that means I'm really assuming. — 17

Now I'm someone else. — 18

Now, again. — 19

I heard today that Alexander Graham Bell did not actually invent the telephone. He stole an essential idea for it from someone else. I heard that on the radio. — 20

A curator recently told me it would be very useful to my career if I stayed young-looking for the next five years. — 21

She wasn't being rude, actually, just pragmatic. — 22

Another book that broke me open again was *The Political Unconscious.* — 23

24   I'm running out of things to say.

25   I wish I could borrow a random thing from someone else.

xvi

1   Once when I was crossing Schubert Alley on 44th Street in NY, I saw Ethel Merman crossing the street. Then I heard loud music and she burst into song, singing "Everything's Coming Up Roses."

2   They were shooting a TV special. I must have been 17 years old. There's no business like show business.

3   The hardest thing about a random list is getting started.

4   For a while I loved nothing more than Broadway musicals. I went once a week with my boyfriend from high school. We got rush tickets, half-price and standing room.

5   Very soon I found all of that embarrassing, and then I repressed my extensive knowledge of the repertoire of American musical theater. It's like no business I know.

6   When I am outside and alone, I can focus completely on the natural world, especially plants, and detach from human things.

7   I had intense relations to certain plants as a child. Marigolds, pine trees, and daylilies spring to mind.

8   I was in psychoanalysis for two years, but I did not really believe in its power until one day I came slightly late and the door was locked. After a minute, I realized that my analyst was mad at me for being late, and I began to cry. Then she showed

up and told me she had just had a car accident and would have to cancel our session. And then I was so worried about her, I really started sobbing.

After I realized there was a whole system of naming plants with Latin names like *Hemerocallis fulva*, I had to learn the Latin name of every plant around me.

9

To this day I feel as if I don't really know a plant until I know its name.

10

Two months ago I went to the Freud Museum in London. I spent about 45 minutes staring at his couch, which is displayed in his office the way it was when he died in 1939.

11

It was all I could do not to jump the barrier and take a running dive onto it.

12

Have you noticed that torn clothes are not cool anymore? They were only cool when the economy was good.

13

I didn't actually notice this myself. David and Austin did, but I wrote it down.

14

In order to keep random, I am taking notes whenever I can. So my whole day is random. It doesn't just have to be a random hour.

15

You can harvest things randomly.

16

I'm adopting a random style.

17

There was a time in my life when I did nothing except eat, sleep, have sex, and look for sex. Kind of in reverse order though.

18

In high school I was a stage-door Johnny. My boyfriend and I waited outside the theaters to get the actors to autograph our *Playbills*.

19

20   We saw *Equus* once with Richard Burton and then got his autograph as he left the theater with Suzy Hunt, whom he dated after he broke up with Liz Taylor the second time.

21   Suzy Hunt was still married to her husband, a race car driver.

22   Why do I remember stuff like this?

23   I haven't talked about my family or my mother for a while.

24   What about that phrase, a plant in the audience?

25   I always imagine a real plant on a folding chair.

xvii

1   For a while I had this theory that literature was basically a hybrid of two simple things: gossip and confessions.

2   The thing about gossip isn't really the inappropriate or invasive information you pass from one person to the other, but the conspiratorial bond you create by saying or hearing something you're not supposed to.

3   And the rest is confession. All the personal parts, the parts about you.

4   It's interesting that in return for a confession you get absolution. You have to give up the bad thing about yourself in order to be saved.

5   But who is the confessor?

6   The other night I had tacos from a Korean taco truck not far from my house. There was a big line. It's a real LA thing, mixing ethnic cuisines.

The suffering of the rich is not like the suffering of the poor.   7

David Wright overheard his sister, who owns a house and is a high school principal who can't lose her job, telling her two kids that times are hard and they really need to economize.   8

I love David Wright.   9

In *The Wretched of the Earth*, Frantz Fanon says there is a necessity of violence for the colonized. He calls this violence a cleansing force.   10

Deep down inside almost all the beautiful people I've known have felt that beauty was as much a barrier as an advantage.   11

I lived in Koreatown during the Rodney King riots and, on the worst day, I decided to leave before the curfew at sundown. Three blocks from my house someone threw a rock at my car and cracked my windshield.   12

A day before that, at UCLA, while smoke from the fires covered the city, I had sex with an architecture student in the men's bathroom.   13

I love apples, which, when they are good, are the mangos of the temperate world.   14

When the riots started, I don't think I was the only person, the only white person, who was somehow elated. I don't think I was the only white person who thought, Yes, finally!   15

How did David Letterman turn into such a bitter person? I remember when he was young and irreverent, sort of a funny outsider. Now he's like Johnny Carson, who I always hated. Mean, powerful, and resentful.   16

17   After George Bush was elected, there was a book published called *Sore Winners*. It was about the resentment of privileged people who acquire great power and still feel put upon.

18   "I've been to paradise but I've never been to me."
      – Charlene

19   I have a great old Danish Modern sofa. It's covered in a mid-green, nubby wool fabric, but smells bad and is stained with pee from my old, incontinent dog, Peggy.

20   It does not disgust me, though I avoid it. I'm keeping it until Peggy dies, which I don't think will be very far off.

21   Chairs can have a lot of integrity.

22   How can you talk about 9/11, watching it on TV super early in LA and watching those buildings go down?

23   All those people.

24   With a few exceptions, I think the sofa is one of the most ugly forms of furniture.

25   The best piece of writing I ever read about 9/11 was by Russel Swensen. He described the bodies falling from the towers like punctuation marks, like commas.

xviii

1   The most beautiful man I ever saw was Adriano Pedrosa. I mean the most beautiful man I talked to, who was actually talking to me.

2   Or David Burns. His beauty was not just in how he looked, but how he looked at you.

Every most beautiful person you see is the most beautiful person you see. 3

In the same manner I still love all the people I loved once, and all in the same way as I did then. 4

The first time I saw Kathy Acker after she had her mastectomy, she lifted up her shirt to show me her scars. 5

I have nothing to say now. 6

When I feel this, I think of being in psychoanalysis for two years. There's no such thing as nothing there. Nothing means something. 7

There's always something behind nothing. Resistance, or flows. 8

If I tell you things about me, you will be able to control me. 9 ✳

I saw Christo's umbrellas the day before one blew over and killed a woman, and they shut them down permanently. 10

I thought I'd hate the umbrellas, but I ended up liking them. 11

What kept me from getting onto Freud's couch in his museum in London was not knowing if I wanted to face out on it or dive in head first. 12

In other words, should the good doctor solve the problems in my heart or in my head? 13

It's a truism that the world rewards writers who work in a consistent style and with consistent content over a long period. 14

I am constitutionally incapable of doing this. 15

16   For most of my life, I've had trouble just completing an internally consistent long project.

17   Sometimes I see people I know on gay cruising sites online.

18   I like the word content, how it means two things, at least. Happy or full of substance.

19   Maybe there's a link: to be happy you need to be filled with something. Not empty.

20   One of the first places I was published was in an anthology called *Discontents,* edited by Dennis Cooper. That's not really a word but you get it: dissent, dissident, malcontents.

21   I would torture my brother by spreading out all the blankets on top of each other and then making him lie down on them. I'd roll him back and forth until he was wrapped thick inside them. Then I'd take two belts and tie him around the arms and the feet and leave him lying there.

22   I think the piece I wrote for *Discontents* was actually some kind of list.

23   Writing random things for so many days every day is similar to being in analysis. All your life in fragments, parts relating to wholes.

24   I am so sick of talking about myself.

25   You start to see how writing is an empty exercise in pushing around pieces to look like a whole thing.

xix

1   Connie Samaras asked me what I thought of Žižek, and I told her I thought he was a dildo. He's a pundit, but he's also strategic. He satisfies

our need for intellectuals to talk to us in our own cartoonish voice, with illustrations from Hitchcock or Disney.

Why can't people read Marx or Freud anymore? Or Lacan? 2

I will use these random things to lodge all my complaints against the world. 3

In India they have hundreds of varieties of mangos, and they all taste different. I can't tell you how excited this gets me. 4 ✳

For many years my father worked at 48 West 48th Street, overlooking Rockefeller Center. In the winter you could see the ice skaters. 5

Everyone gets to be the most beautiful person once in their life, although sometimes no one is around to see it. 6

The thing I liked about *Einstein on the Beach* the first time I saw it was how it made me understand that a work of art could be empty and slow. 7

Did I set out to have sexual adventures? 8

Absolutely. 9

I'm still thinking about the Pipilotti Rist video installation I saw at MOMA. So big and empty. But very decorative. Psychedelic, like a dream state, or following the sort of dream logic in Hollywood animated films. 10

People were really loving it, hundreds of them, just lounging around on the big, circular sofa. 11

The most dangerous person I've ever known is Sande Cohen. We used to wonder if he was crazy 12 or evil or both, until it became clear that it didn't matter.

13 Sande's problem is that his critique of institutions and disciplines is obscured by his need for recognition and authority.

14 I don't think anyone is really beautiful unless I can see or imagine or project that they have a brain.

15 When I sense Sande's presence in the office next to mine, I take a plastic saber (from Halloween) and set it pointed in his direction. As if all his evil intentions land on the knife and only hurt him.

16 I'll use magical thinking when it seems useful. Yup.

17 I'd rather be a hammer than a nail.

18 In general, I want more information than I require. I will spend hours researching a thing in the library or on the internet.

19 Information has content. In German the word is *inhalt*.

20 We are biased in favor of the information that exists over the information that does not exist.

21 Judie Bamber posted a meme in which you're supposed to Google "[your name] needs" and list the first ten results.

22 Matias needs to sell just over 9000 keyboards to use up the promised million keyswitches. Matias needs new numbers! Matias needs to move I think, he needs change. Matias needs a photo to post. Send Matias a photo. I see that Matias needs to make some of the elements of the images a bit darker in this respect. Matias needs to do less volunteering and more work for pay. Matias

needs to SHUT UP! Matias needs a host family from December to April. Matias needs a while to get himself up to scratch.

Mine was very different from hers, and the most noticeable thing was gender.   23

So I ran "butch needs," which was pretty great.   24
Then femme needs. And sinners need, no one needs; everyone, someone, we all, God, the earth, and Facebook addicts need.

Who knew there was so much need in the world?   25

xx

For many years, my parents refused to get a   1
TV. They were immune to my brother's and my complaints ("people think we're poor!"), and they only did get one because they were losing their kids to all the neighbors.

All I can remember watching are *I Dream of*   2
Genie, *Bewitched*, and *I Love Lucy*. In some way you could say they were all the same show. Nutty women and their harried men. That's what defined America for me, the freaks against the normal people.

"And I'm working at trying to find a kind of   3
language where I won't be so easily modulated by expectation." – Kathy Acker

A few years after we got a TV, my cousin   4
Susana stayed with us after she emigrated from Argentina. She spoke some English, but basically she learned about America by watching re-runs of *Love, American Style* with me.

Peggy sheds much more than you'd imagine,   5
and, because she is a Dalmatian, her hair is either

black or white, which means it doesn't blend in to anything.

6   You have to wonder how the Flarf writers and the Language Poets feel about all this meme stuff, all these lists, these texts from Google searches, etc. Does it raise the value of what they're doing, or does it level it?

7   For a long time I didn't particularly like men with beards, but then I met Brian Blanchfield and got a crush on him and since then I really like them.

8   I have a beard now myself.

9   And all the writers doing constrained work or procedural work or the New York School—are they being elevated or diminished?

10   I know we watched all the "good" TV shows like *All in the Family* and *Maude,* but I only remember the bad shows.

11   If generating random things about yourself is anything like therapy, maybe when times get really hard people will make lists instead.

12   Making a list is not the same as writing about yourself. You have more defenses when you're talking about your problems and complaints. Like when you're telling a story.

13   I feel very naked right now.

14   In this text I can identify several elements of tragedy and comedy, but also lyric and epic things. In the end, I'm afraid it's all melodrama. Melodrama has all the elements above, but no respect for any of them.

15   This is kitsch.

For the most part, I grew up on Staten Island: 16
woods, suburbs, and urban blight side by side.

I used to dream of going to Manhattan on the 17
ferry. As we got closer, the water would turn
turquoise, and dolphins or flying fish would leap
out of the water. I'd be so impatient I'd jump off
the boat and swim to the city, which had turned
into a tropical paradise.

The Depression was really hard on a lot of people. 18
Except, when you think about it, not a lot of
people were actually killed by it.

Random: could be anything, but usually isn't. 19

Things: we're biased in favor of tangibility. Things 20
need to look like things for us to recognize them.
Even partial things, parts, we want them to point
at whole things.

About: the question of the subject. What pertains 21
to me? What is close by, in some proximity?

Me: ugh. 22

Too: everyone is doing these random lists. All we 23
can learn from them is how suggestible we are.

25: one quarter of 100, the tenth square number. 24
Part of the whole. Two bits.

I once had sex standing up in a sex club in 25
Amsterdam with my boyfriend and a guy we met
there.

xxi

Often when I am waiting in an airport, I will poke 1
at my luggage and find some of my dog's hair. I
stuff it into a crevice of the airport furniture.

2   This way she travels all over the world and pieces of her are left everywhere. Maybe they will outlast us both.

3   This project feels increasingly formulaic. There's nothing new here. Isn't writing supposed to "make it new"?

4   It's like a combination of John Cage and Joe Brainard, writing yourself out in bits and pieces.

5   Both of them were gay too. Can a gay man's life only be told in random fragments?

6   My favorite nail to bite is my pointer finger, and then my thumb.

7   The one time in history when the fragment was really valued was during the Romantic period.

8   The best random things come when I am furthest from a piece of paper or my keyboard.

9   I usually forget them.

10   Where do they go?

11   When I was trapped in long lines in the post office, I used to look around and make a list of who I'd sleep with first, then next, all the way to last, if I had to.

12   Sedona, Arizona.

13   After I went to college, one of my friends who was still in high school brought me her friend, Adam Schwerner. Adam thought he might be gay, and we decided I would tutor him a little, to see if he was.

Adam slept over a few times, and once we went 14
to the Zen Center in the Bronx with his father,
Armand, a poet, who treated me very sweetly
even though I was his seventeen-year-old son's
legally adult boyfriend.

I tend to like apples more than oranges. I like any 15
fruit with more than just a monoflavor. A fruit
with depth.

Adam was a sexy boy with wavy, longish blond 16
hair. At that time, a year's age difference seemed
enormous.

Some fruits have biflavors, or triflavors. Think of 17
grapefruits, or pears. With the best fruit you can
barely identify the range of components.

You can make a kind of argument around the 18
benefits and liabilities of monogamy, but I won't.

Leslie Dick spent a day upset about not finding 19
the first volume of Virginia Woolf's letters. She
thought maybe someone borrowed it and didn't
bring it back; she couldn't remember anything
more about it.

Few things fill me with as much angst and 20
existential unease as not finding a book I know I
have. (I feel as if a child is being beaten!)

There is another thing going around online where 21
you find your porn name by combining the name
of your first pet with the street you lived on as
kid, which makes my porn name Fluffy City.

The meme: me me. 22

I haven't really talked about my family in a while. 23
I'd like to think that means I'm done with them,
but I know it probably means the opposite.

24 I believe there is a psychic equation between depression and anger, that depressed people are often attracted to angry ones, and vice versa.

25 I love to use the word psychic not in its ESP sense.

xxii

1 In 1973 I went back to Argentina with my father for the first time since we emigrated. We got there the day after Perón came back from his eighteen year exile. There had been a riot at the airport when the right-wing Perónists fired on the crowd of three million so-called leftist Perónists who were there to welcome him.

2 Thirteen people were killed. When we landed, we didn't know what had happened. The airport was covered in litter and paper. I remember being shocked by the mess.

3 A week later, my father and I were caught in a riot. People were racing down the street throwing things and breaking windows. My father covered me and pulled me into a doorway. Near us a car was burning, and I was sure I saw a person inside banging at the windows.

4 I asked my father about this not long ago; he does not remember a person in the car.

5 Did I make this up? Is it something I saw in a movie? That's how I remember it, like a movie.

6 David Burns knows this system by which every day of the year translates into playing cards, and each one has a meaning. He says that my birthday makes me the King of Clubs. The king has the burden of leadership. He already has everything he needs, but he needs to learn how to use it and to get people to help him. Even kings need help.

In my life I can see the second part, but not the   7
burden of leadership. I probably already have most
of what I need, but I need to learn how to use it.

The other day a pebble flew into my windshield   8
and made a crack in the form of a little x. I was
driving to work and I was late because I had to
stop at Mady Schutzman's house to drop off some
fruit trees.

I already felt bad because I was late to Mady's—I   9
had meant to come the day before—and then
I was late to school. I felt as if the x on my
windshield was some kind of mark against me. It
was almost at eye level.

At the end of the day today, I walked outside   10
CalArts around sunset, and the clouds were
streaked back and forth by jet trails. Right above
me was a gigantic x, as if to say you are here.

X marks the spot.   11

It was beautiful but also ominous. I was waiting   12
for a third x, an even bigger sign from the
universe, but it never came.

I once had sex at Limelight in NY, in the little   13
room way upstairs. Limelight was a club they had
in a converted church. It was hip, and then for a
long time, it was really nasty.

What must it have been like for my parents to   14
emigrate twice in one lifetime, to leave one
continent for another, and then for yet another?

There's an old question about the purpose of art: is   15
it to make you see or to make you feel something?

And then people started to ask, what about   16
thinking? Why can't art make you think?

17   And if you put sex in it, suddenly it's not art, but pornography. Kind of like seeing and feeling, but more dangerous: sensing and arousal. It's the opposite of thinking altogether, to most people.

18   So the most unlikely thing would be work that makes you think about sex.

19   I remember getting on the elevator with my father at his office on 48th Street, and suddenly he was speaking in a language I didn't recognize with the Jewish men in black coats.

20   It was Yiddish.

21   Fifteen years ago, at a great low in my life, I took a road trip by myself to Sedona, Arizona. I'd read about how the whole town was an energy vortex and I thought if I went there I could fix myself.

22   On the first night, I camped out in the woods and immediately felt better, but I wanted a bed, so I went to the health food store and found a place to rent listed on the store's bulletin board. The house belonged to a psychic woman who stayed up all night transcribing transmissions she received from other galaxies. She showed me her notebooks filled with the alien language, and all her diagrams and sketches of their world.

23   In the morning, she offered to do a past-life regression with me so I could learn where all my blockages came from and how to clear them.

24   People party, take drugs, and have sex in former churches.

25   Robert Smithson's *Spiral Jetty*.

xxiii

There is human time, and then there is geological time, and finally astronomic time, the biggest time of all. One is very small, one is very big, and the other is in between.   1

My parents were older than all my friends' parents, and it embarrassed me.   2

A few times people thought my father was my grandfather.   3

They were old and they spoke English with an accent, and that was pretty much enough to hold against them for a while.   4

The only earthwork marked on a US topographical map is Nancy Holt's *Sun Tunnels*, which are these four huge pipes aligned in an x so that at each solstice you can see the sun rising and setting through different pipes.   5

An astrologer told my mother she would have two sons and live on three continents. This was just before my mother got married, and the astrologer was friends with my father's family.   6

The odds were, for a postwar woman, that she'd have two kids, so two boys is a one out of four likelihood. She had met my father in Germany, but they were going back to Argentina, so two continents was hardly a guess at all, though at the time the notion that someone would switch continents a second time was unlikely. I'd give that a one out of four too. Maybe he saw a restless quality in my mother or father.   7

So the odds for his entire prediction coming true were at least one in sixteen.   8

9   I'm not very good at math, though for many years in school, math was my best subject. I remember making a determined decision to be better at English than at math.

10   My mother never saw any kind of psychic or astrologer again.

11   For a few years, I was a sort of performance artist, but after a while it wasn't interesting to me anymore. Too much of it was like sitcoms on TV.

12   I maintain that the letters t, y, and s are the basic difference between poetry and prose. The only word these letters form is sty, which means that trying to locate this difference is either very dirty or a form of visual impairment.

13   Probably everyone knows this, but the word "poetry" didn't really mean what it means today until after the word "prose" was coined. Before then, poetry just meant literary writing.

14   "Heterosexual" didn't come into use until "homosexual" was coined.

15   Perhaps this means there is something very gay about prose.

16   There was something remarkable about just sitting in the vortexes of Sedona and gazing at the beautiful red rocks, mesas, and buttes. People say there's a geomagnetic force from the iron in the ground, which also makes it turn so red.

17   Do I change the order of my random things before I finish with them each day?

18   Doesn't everyone?

19   I am certain I saw Katherine Hepburn once on the subway in NY. She was famously cheap and

did things like take the subway. She seemed to be trembling (she already had Parkinson's), and she had a scarf around her head and part of her face. If it wasn't her, it was someone who wanted to be mistaken for her.

As I think about this, I seem to remember she had   20
a bicycle with her on the train. But if she was so old and shaky, how was that possible?

So the bicycle must be from a dream or something   21
I read, but if that's the case, how can I be sure I remember seeing her at all?

In my going-to-theater days I saw Katherine   22
Hepburn on stage in a play called *A Matter of Gravity*.

There was a spell when my favorite fruit was one   23
particular brand of canned lychees. Now it's hard to imagine.

All those *Playbills* I saved, so many of them with   24
autographs, where are they now?

Most of my things up to my college years were   25
in my parents' house, but after my mother died and my father moved out I could not deal with anything, so someone probably threw them away.

xxiv

There are things I prefer not to remember.   1

Whenever my mother heard sirens, close or far,   2
she would stiffen up, freeze somehow, and glaze over.

We talked about the War in my family, but never   3
about what actually happened to my mother or father. They wanted us to know about the War, but not about anything that happened to them.

4   Why did my father let us get caught in a riot, what were we doing out that night, why does he think I didn't see what I think I saw?

5   Egg whites stiffen best in a copper bowl. My mother believed that.

6   My favorite rhyme for the word "sex" is probably "checks," though "ex" and "vortex" and, of course, "complex" are appealing.

7   That was the thing about Vorticism, to capture the movement in an image. Let nothing sit still.

8   And my favorite sex organ is, of course, the cerebral cortex.

9   I remember the first game I learned in the United States as a kid. It was tag.

10   When I think of that now, what I notice most is it. You're it. What is this it? In German it is *es*, the word Freud used for the id. Formless, dark, immeasurable.

11   Being it. Occupying the space of it.

12   Tonight I looked at Justin Underhill's photos. Nice. He's a twin. I really know his brother, Jason; I have never met Justin.

13   It's the twin thing. Like the Wertheims, only those sisters are actually identical. Which is why I like calling them the Sisters Wertheim.

14   I noticed Justin Underhill is friends with other Justin Underhills.

15   This is a form of communion you miss as Matias Viegener. I am the only Matias Viegener in the world, or rather, on the internet. It's a solitary

thing, my name. Compare it to Vanessa Place, who has the comfort of both company and location.

And names like Underhill, they always make me want to find an Overhill. Some names set doors swinging in a person's mind. 16

Are all your friends joking about poverty and homelessness? 17

A few days ago I wrote the name of a random place: Sedona, Arizona. The word probably came into my head from its weird internal rhyme, like Chevy Nova, which I remember once repeating to myself over and over until it became Chevanova. I liked that one place name, just a random mark, nothing discursive, no story or meaning. 18

But then it became a story. 19

I saw Laurie Anderson in the St. Mark's Bookshop once. She's tiny. 20

[Random thing removed for observation.] 21

Right now I feel the anxiety of too much to say and not enough. 22

Everyone is trapped by form in some way, but only some of us are trapped by the excessive consciousness of form. 23

I feel like the only way I can end this list is with the death of my mother. 24

No one knows what it is to be it naturally. We all needed to be trained. 25

XXV

I have often blundered in the direction of defending people I felt were under attack, only to 1 hurt those who weren't actually attacking them. You know who you are.

2   Already six people are listed as dead from yesterday's blizzard in the Northeast. It is interesting to compare the number of people killed by weather in the East to the number killed by earthquakes in California. And yet California is seen as a dangerous place to live.

3   I wrote ganderous instead of dangerous. But I already fixed it.

4   The rioters were mostly men, chanting, "Perón, Perón." In their very deep voices, it sounded like PAY-RUN, PAY-RUN. Not so much a name as a command, the deep voice of the unconscious.

5   In high school I read *The Descent of Woman* by Elaine Morgan. Her theory was that primal humans lived for a while in the water, which is how we got to be naked apes with relatively little hair.

6   I am learning how many random thoughts I have in a day that surface only to be submerged again.

7   This teaches you to be attentive.

8   When you're in a collaboration, you forget your own ideas much less easily. Maybe because you know that in some part it's a constant struggle to be heard, and if you don't remember, no one else will.

9   Snow Days, just the words "Snow Days."

10 I remember walking down Broadway from 116th Street to Times Square, the city covered in snow, not one car.

Christine Wertheim is opposed to Facebook on the 11
grounds that it represents another "orifice" through
which we must pass things in and out. She believes
we modern people have too many orifices already,
and that at some point it all starts to hurt.

Peggy's whole body is moving to rub her nose 12
on the carpet, and it causes her to groan with
pleasure.

Everything comes to an end, and the end is what 13
defines the thing. The end of the trail.

It's only death that finally comes to define life. 14

My mother didn't "know" she died; she went into 15
a coma. I knew, though, so she knew too, if you
understand what I mean.

I remember patchouli. 16

Jason Underhill did an independent study with 17
me, and a few times we talked about Justin, his
twin brother who was gay. I think it was because
I was gay, so there was a kind of context, and
I'm a brother, though not a twin. But sometimes
people thought my brother was my twin and I
distinctly did not like that.

The key letter of the word twin is w. It's the joint, 18
or double nature, of that letter, the double-u.

Why do Americans love ice cubes so much? 19

What were we doing out the night of the riot in 20
1973? I think we were visiting my father's friends,
the Oesterhelds. Hector Oesterheld, the father,
wasn't there. He was in prison, as was one of the
daughters. Elsa, his wife, made us a nice dinner,
but I noticed that the walls were chipped and the
sofa had a hole.

21 In two years, all four daughters and the father were in prison and we learned over time that all of them had been killed, their bodies dumped in the South Atlantic. Two of the daughters' babies were taken by other families.

22 The Oesterhelds were my godparents. Hector wrote graphic novels. A journalist was told the government killed him "because he wrote the most beautiful story of Che Guevara ever written."

23 Two years ago in Argentina I saw Elsa and met her grandson Fernando—one of the children they got back from his adoptive family. He gave me a new edition of the Che book.

24 Peggy is all nose.

25 One day I will translate the Che book into English.

xxvi

1 I snore.

2 In one of the vitrines in the Evita museum in Buenos Aires, you will find a glass syringe once used to inject Evita with drugs as she was dying of cancer.

3 I knew Carolee Schneemann for a few years, but I didn't really get to know her until she stayed at my house. She was teaching a workshop at CalArts, and she got thrown out of the visiting artist suite because of her cat, Treasure, who traveled everywhere with her.

4 My neighbors remember Carolee Schneemann because, after the cat disappeared for a few hours, she stood outside all night long wailing his name, "Treasure! Treasure!"

I like bitter things.   5

Treasure was the reincarnation of Vesper, and   6
after Treasure died, Carolee sent me an email
saying she had located the next reincarnation not
far from her in upstate New York.

Umami is the flavor of meatiness, the   7
proteinaceous, like Parmesan cheese, grilled meat,
pickled herring, sautéed mushrooms.

I tasted it before I knew about it, but I didn't   8
know. You think you know all the flavors—sweet,
sour, salty and bitter—but then there is another.

This is why binary systems are usually insufficient.

At a certain point my dog made it much harder   9
for me to hook up with guys on the internet. I'd
look at her and think: do I want to get in bed
with her or with some guy I don't know on the
other side of town? She wins almost every time.

My cousin Susana took a photograph of the two   10
of us standing in front of Evita's tomb in the
Recoleta cemetery, smiling.

This is an exercise in letting go. For so long I   11
have held tight to my ideas, my stories, and my
theories.

Stapelias are succulents with large, fleshy, drab,   12
star-shaped flowers that smell like rotting meat.
They imitate carrion in order to attract pollinating
flies.

I just looked at Noah Webb's photos of Big Sur,   13
photos of Noah photographing Big Sur. There
was some kind of blob of plastic hanging down
the tripod from the bottom of the camera, like
ectoplasm.

14   I looked that up after I wrote it. Ectoplasm: a supernatural, viscous substance.

15   My parents grew up in the Depression, and they had some of the typical habits of that generation, so I feel like I've been well-prepared for what times may come.

16   *The Secret Life of Plants* is one of the first books I can remember reading.

17   I watched the famous OJ Simpson car chase on TV with a big crowd in the St. Mark's Bookshop.

18   It was so NY. Also, so LA.

19   The "it" or id is formless, dark, and immeasurable, a perfect subject for fiction.

20   It's hard to explain you're not just German, you're Jewish too. Especially when your family doesn't want to talk about any of it.

21   Another book that was very powerful to me was B.F. Skinner's *Walden Two*, which I read before Thoreau's *Walden*. All I remember about it now was that the kids were raised communally. All the kids I knew were reading it.

22   Also there is something called a Skinner Box that is used for lab experiments with mice. At some point, it got muddled in my head with Cornell boxes, which are not at all the same thing.

23   Yes, I still have that terrible sinus headache.

24   My thermostat has four settings for different times of the day: evening, night, morning, and day. It's made for working people who only need heat when they get home from work and when they get up for work, so they don't waste money heating when they are asleep or away.

It took me years to understand this.   25

xxvii

There's a certain style of gardening I've come to   1
embrace. I call it Darwinian. A kind of survival of
the fittest, no tears for the precious dead.

You can see conceptual art as being at its core a   2
kind of "aesthetics of administration" rather than
creative subjectivity or expression: you set up a
paradigm or hypothesis, and then you follow it
through with some kind of systematicity.

I run the heat all day when I am away. I do it for   3
my dog who's old and starts shivering sometimes
for no obvious reason.

Tehching Hsieh was a performance artist who   4
punched a time clock every hour on the hour
for one year in 1980. At night he woke up every
hour. He also took a picture of himself each time
he punched the time clock, so you can watch his
hair grow for a year.

I noticed that on his early material he calls himself   5
Sam Hsieh, and then he changed his name back
at some point.

He also lived outside for a year, spent a year locked   6
in a wooden cage (you can see that cage right now
at the Museum of Modern Art in NY), and used
a rope to tie himself to Linda Montano for a year.

Tehching sounds to me like the punch of the time   7
clock, or a cash register.

I always wondered if Michael Schwerner (one of   8
the three civil rights workers killed in Mississippi
by the KKK in 1964, in a famous murder case)
was related to Adam and Armand Schwerner.

9   When I said earlier that the Depression didn't actually kill anyone, I think I was wrong. It's more like cancer. Cancer itself doesn't really kill you, but the consequences sometimes or often do.

10   Tehching.

11   When I was young I came up with a title of something to write, but I never figured out what it should be. The title was *A Streaker Named Desire*.

12   Within the space of a year, I visited the city I was born, Buenos Aires; the house where I grew up, in Staten Island; and my furthest flung relative, in New Zealand. I wasn't really searching to connect anything, but still it's interesting that, in the end, none of it really connected.

13   Is it wrong of me to be happy when my lists online get a lot of comments? If not, is it wrong to be unhappy when they don't get any?

14   Carolee Schneemann has a whole bunch of cat videos that she's made in the last ten years that people seem to hate. Many of them are about her obsessive relationships with her cats, including Vesper, the kissing cat, with lots of shots of her kissing him, with tongue, on the mouth.

15   Suddenly I'm feeling a lot of resistance here.

16   As if something is expected of me.

17   I'm not coming up with the confessional goods.

18   I am fascinated with Schneemann's cat work. To me it seems as radical as her work in the 1960s, only about interspecies relationships instead of gender.

19   And I'm obviously stalling.

In Buenos Aires, you should never go to the tango   20
places for tourists, but definitely to the milongas,
which are tango places for amateurs. I went to the
Confiteria Ideal with Jen Hofer and her family,
which is in a huge 19th-century cafe that has seen
better days. The dancers are like oil, all surface,
one pose after another, cold as ice, but hot too.

I was lucky to be able to become a Hofer very   21
quickly. Usually the application process is
protracted, but the Hofers took to me, and the
circumstances were good: being in Buenos Aires
where Jen's father grew up and I was born but
didn't grow up.

I used to be jealous of Ken Ehrlich because he   22
became a Hofer long ago.

On the same trip I got to know my cousin's best   23
friend, Wolfram, who grew up there; a model,
then an actor, and now a psychoanalyst. Jen's
mother, also a shrink (like Jen's father!), found
Wolfram's name very funny and could hardly
contain herself. It doesn't have the same wolfish
ring in Spanish though.

Someone tried to give me a Pooh Hug through   24
the Hug Me application on Facebook. I don't
want a Pooh Hug. Nor do I want an Easter egg, or
a "plant." And why is everyone poking everyone
else? What's wrong with hello?

I was tempted by the Frida Kahlo gifts, and the   25
regalitos revolucionarios, and even the punk rock
singles requests, but once you start down that
road, what's to stop you?

xxviii

Noah Webb is a handsome man. I've noticed over   1
the years there's a kind of syndrome of handsome

gay men who become photographers. You have to wonder what it means.

2   There's also Marc Geller. And Matthew Rolston. Even Mapplethorpe.

3   Taking photographs is a way of controlling the gaze instead of being its focus.

4   My mother was trained as a photographer but gave it up. She photographed every broken barn she found in New York and New England. She loved the way they collapsed.

5   Carolee Schneemann told Linda Frye Burnham that the best thing about her cat was that it liked to give "catilingus."

6   My parents had an appreciation for certain things about American culture. Wooden duck decoys. Moonshine jugs. Collapsed barns. These must all sound like the clichés of Americana, but through my mother I came to see them as very exotic.

7   They were pretty unmoved by other pieces of Americana of the time, like quilts, but they did like Warhol, especially the soup cans.

8   Something about Tehching Hsieh being Sam for a while in the 70s touches me. It feels so immigrant.

9   I have never held a stock in my life.

10   My cold has moved from my sinuses to my throat and chest. Sometimes I'm not sure if the cold inhabits you, or if you inhabit the cold.

11   There's a new word I saw today: *Fleischgeist*. Like *Zeitgeist*, the spirit of the times, but meaning the spirit of the meat, the idea of the meat.

As a teenager, maybe at 14, I would write these romantic poems, but always in fragments. 12

I wasn't sure how to finish them, or if I wanted to. 13

Most of them I burned around the edges so they would look as though someone had pulled them from a fire at the last minute. 14

There were always cigarette lighters in the house. 15

A little earlier, at 12 or so, I was obsessed with a Danish poet who wrote these little rhymes called *Grooks*. I had every volume. 16

If you look him up now, you will see that he writes what could fairly be called doggerel. 17

"Everything's either / concave or convex, / so whatever you dream / will be something with sex." 18

Piet Hein. All his books are out of print now, but this summer, when I am in Copenhagen, I will look for his memorial. 19

At the core of Tehching Hsieh and On Kawara's work is the concept of duration. 20

I learned about them from Barbara Campbell and her *1001 Nights Cast*, where she read a story every night for 1001 nights on a webcast. Without fail. 21

Maybe durational performance becomes more meaningful in our time because the world pulls at us so much. 22

There was a period when I needed to believe in UFOs and astrology. I read *Sun Signs*. 23

I hated Ayn Rand. And the *Hobbit* books. Even though all the other kids were reading them. 24

25   And John Updike's *Rabbit* books, even though they had sex, like *The Godfather*, which everyone passed around.

xxix

1   My parents hated Evita and Perón and all of what they stood for. They also hated tango. I think somehow the two were linked in their minds.

2   Long ago I got my parents tickets to see *Evita*, thinking they would want to see it. They actually liked it, but said it was all kitsch. First they lived it, then they had to live through the musical.

3   For me there are tides for random things, high and low. Spring tides and neap tides. Nothing random about it. If I keep going, everything I think is random will recur and then you will find a pattern. Duration exhausts randomness.

4   Thinking versus sex. We think of them as opposites; thinking is not sexy, and sex is about sensation and maybe delirium, but not thinking.

5   Smells too. Can smells make us think?

6   I think Dennis Cooper's books are actually about philosophy: truth, beauty, desire and death, all in the language of a fucked-up Californian teenager.

7   There's a whole theme of mixed blood in Thomas Mann. The *Mischling*. The Germanic and the Latin. Tonio Kröger feels both superior to the burghers in his insights and envious of their innocent vitality.

8   You have to wonder how much lower the stock market can go.

I have a smell on my wrist right now. I can't describe it except in a word, one word: Araby. 9

For a long time I've loved the work of Bas Jan Ader, but it's not really his work exactly. A part of it is how he disappeared in a sailboat in the Atlantic, sailing back to Europe. The sail was part of a piece called *In Search of the Miraculous*. 10

All his work is mute in some way: silent films in which he falls from a roof in Los Angeles, rides his bike into a canal in Amsterdam, or dangles from a branch over a pond until he falls in. 11

Every time I've gone to Amsterdam, I've looked for that canal. 12

There's the feeling of ectoplasm again. Like 19th-century spirit photography. Who wouldn't be interested? 13

It's rare to find such an overlap of art and life. 14

I remember going to visit my brother's girlfriend, Marie, at a psychiatric hospital in upstate New York. He and I went together. She had some kind of breakdown from alcohol toxicity. 15

I'd like to make a list of everyone's political and religious views from Facebook. 16

For several months, David Burns was into bird omens. I can't leave the house today, he'd say. I saw three sparrows on a fence, and two left. 17

An augur is a reader of bird omens, also called auspices. 18

Plato says that even more valued than augury was hepatoscopy: reading the liver of a sacrificial victim. 19

20 My lists are a combination of megalomania and trivial pursuits. Though maybe that is the same thing. I hate trivia, actually.

21 I always thought the *Hobbit* books were a kind of medieval kitsch—false, plodding, and dull.

22 Maybe this is because my bedtime reading as a child came from volumes of folk tales and fairy tales, many of them from my grandparents' house.

23 Grimm's tales, Greek myths, Viking folklore, and other folklore too: Indian, Irish, Sanskrit, etc.

24 Rumpelstiltskin is my name.

25 I just had dinner at James McHugh's house, and before I left, he put these fragrant Indian oils on my hands, and now I feel intoxicated.

xxx

1 My childhood until age 5 could almost have been the 19th century. No plastic toys, no TV, no radio even. Just records, mostly classical. Folk and fairy tales.

2 Breastfed, no baby food from a jar. No candy, no soda.

3 I can remember going to a butcher with my mother and her trying to distract me while they cut off the chicken's head.

4 My kitchen is filled with fruit flies; I've let them get out of hand.

5 Paul McCarthy is the only American artist who understands how dismal Christmas can be.

Something about spirit photography had to do   6
with the newly invented camera, how mysterious
it must have seemed.

My brother's name is Valentin.   7

My parents liked the romantic Latin names.   8

Nancy Buchanan says Paul McCarthy "made" Bas   9
Jan Ader famous and that people become famous
because someone with power decides they should
be remembered.

I agree. Individually, we remember anyone we   10
choose, but we can't make them famous unless we
have power to do so.

My mother was fascinating, but unknown.   11

The first time I went to what could be called an   12
orgy was an all-night performance/vigil which was
really a party at Highways for World AIDS Day.

I hear the rush of the furnace, Peggy licking   13
herself, a distant ticking.

Almost anyone we get to know impersonally, like   14
Bas Jan Ader, is already famous somehow, or if
not famous, already "known."

Anyway, famous is not the same as interesting.   15

If you believe in randomness, do you also believe   16
in luck? Or if you believe in luck, do you not
believe in randomness?

David Burns started making pickles lately, fifteen   17
pounds already.

He's also been making frozen bananas.   18

19 But he says there is no pattern to it.

20 I hear a car on the street, an engine maybe from an old American car.

21 Something you notice in Argentina is the ethnic mix of names, like Carlos Messerschmidt or Anneliese Maldonado.

22 I feel that I should like vegetables more than I do.

23 In my family we'd mix German and Spanish expressions, like "*Na ja, mañana.*"

24 In some way Germans and US Americans are more compatible than Germans and Latin-Americans.

25 I hear something ticking.

xxxi

1 A key moment in St. Augustine's *Confessions* is when he talks about stealing pears from his neighbors with some friends, and he realizes, with guilt, that it was less to have the pears than to do something forbidden.

2 In Rousseau's *Confessions* he remembers how he was beaten for stealing apples when he was thirteen years old. When he recalls this, in horror, he drops his pen and can't write.

3 I remember years ago when my brother realized we were going to the same clubs organized by Jim Fouratt, like Danceteria, and for the first time he thought maybe I wasn't so nerdy.

4 In college I had a friend, Chris Radkowski, who later became a Christmas-ornament mogul.

5 He changed his last name to Radko and started having old glass ornaments remanufactured in

Eastern Europe. People wanted them more and more, and in a few years *The New York Times* called him the Czar of Christmas.

I also remember when my brother decided drag queens were cool.   6

One day I saw one of those Dewar's Scotch profiles in a magazine, and it was on Christopher Radko.   7

A year ago or so I saw him for the first time since college, and he told me over dinner that his family's Christmases were actually always unhappy. That was part of his motivation.   8

There's a pop song called "Tempted by the Fruit of Another."   9

Once I fell asleep while visiting Eleanor and David Antin. They put me on a sofa in a bedroom, and it was one of the most intense sleep experiences I've ever had.   10

It was as if I melded with the sofa.   11

I guess Christopher Radko was famous.   12

Those oversized soft drink cups are really disturbing.   13

I saw a shooting star once in Central Park; it was at a Shakespeare in the Park performance.   14

Very dramatic.   15

Another time I saw one while sailing on a schooner in Maine, and another from the beach at night in the Lido di Ostia in Italy. I think it was the "night of the shooting stars," in fact.   16

It's so exciting to see a shooting star.   17

18   Random too.

19   It's like seeing celebrities.

20   There's a jolt when you see celebrities actually exist. Maybe it means you exist too—in a more random, but concrete way.

21   Peggy is shivering, but I don't know why.

22   Once I saw Dolly Parton in a restaurant, Patina. She sat behind me; as soon as I knew she was there, I could feel her vibrations through my chair.

23   She's tiny.

24   I saw Madonna in a Malaysian restaurant on LaBrea once.

25   She looked pretty ratty.

xxxii

1   When we desire someone, do we desire to have them or to be them? That's always an interesting question, maybe more so for gay people.

2   It's a question that came up today in my Queer Books class. But it's a question that won't go away either. And not just for gay people.

3   There are a whole set of my mother's recipes that I lost. Actually, I never wrote them down.

4   I kind of did it on purpose.

5   I thought maybe if I could recreate them they would seem less special, less haunting.

6   One thing I like about teaching is when you teach the same book again, and then a third time, etc.

The same book is different. 7

You see a book is not one thing. It's many things 8
in an arrangement.

And you don't see all the things, or see them evenly, 9
even when that arrangement is simple, or narrative.

In high school, they trained us to read *The New* 10
York Times. They didn't just explain how articles
were placed and what it meant, they showed us
the tricky eight-part fold so you could read the
whole thing seated on a crowded subway.

They were planning on us being successful, but 11
maybe not so successful we wouldn't have to take
the subway.

In Frascati, Italy, you buy roast pork off the spit 12
from a merchant with a big oven, and then you
eat it in a wine cellar where they keep your glass
filled with a beautiful white wine—Frascati it's
called—from the barrel.

There are two kinds of teachers: researchers, 13
always looking for something new, and rehearsers,
who repeat the same things in hopes of maybe
seeing something new.

When you read a book more than once, you see 14
the mechanics of that book.

My mother didn't actually love to cook, she just 15
did it really well.

When you desire someone, there is always a 16
difference between what you think you're getting
and what you get.

Once my boyfriend and I went to visit my 17
parents, and we discovered we both had crabs.

We got the right soap and washed everything, but I decided I should tell my mother just in case the crabs appeared from nowhere after we were gone. She was fine with it. She said during the War everyone had crabs.

18 Of course at rush hour everyone takes the subway. It's the fastest way to get around.

19 When I'm writing 25 random things, I don't think about overall structure. I think about either the sentence or about variety.

20 In a relationship you get: a) more than you want, b) less, or c) other than what you expected.

21 David and Austin don't really understand how little most newspapers mean to me, and how much *The New York Times* does mean to me.

22 I know this is kind of pathetic.

23 I wonder if private-but-public events will change because of Facebook.

24 Rick Moody's wife had a baby, and everyone is leaving him congratulations on his page—often congratulating him but not her. Is that because it's not her page?

25 All the really successful New Yorkers work until 9 or 10 and then get driven home in a limousine.

xxxiii

1 All day I've been thinking of the expression, "Don't hock me a *tshaynik*."

2 It means stop yammering or nagging me.

3 I looked it up, and hock, you've heard, means to nag, but also to bang on something, and *tshaynik* is a teakettle. Stop banging on the kettle.

Kenny Goldsmith says if it's not in *The New York* 4
Times, it doesn't exist.

These are the Yiddish expressions that were used 5
in my family: *nu, nosh, oi veh, oi gevalt, shlep,* and
gonif.

Meat memories: I can remember when I needed 6
to be talked into eating meat as a child. Also with
friends' kids, like Camille, I remember persuading
them to eat their meat.

It's a thing carried from generation to generation. 7

But somewhere in the beginning, there must have 8
been someone who got over their disinclination to
rubbery texture, gristle, and fat, not to mention
the cooked eyeball of their meal looking up at
them.

And funny that for so long, so few have broken 9
that chain.

No, I'm an omnivore. 10

Once in August, Andy and I went up to the house 11
in the mountains and laid on the deck at night to
watch the Perseids meteor shower.

It was freezing, bone-chilling cold. But the sky 12
was combed with shooting stars.

There is an other kind of meat memory, which is 13
lodged in your body: illness, wounds, beatings,
sex. The memory of a kiss.

A *gonif* is like a swindler, a fraud. 14

The only thing I remember about visiting Berlin 15
as a kid is the *Gedächtniskirche*, a bombed-out
church they kept in ruins as a war memorial. And

seeing bullet holes on buildings that still weren't patched, especially on one street near Albert Einstein's house.

16   Only my brother and I, with our Argentine passports, were allowed into East Berlin for a tour. My parents couldn't go.

17   As I said to Russel Swensen earlier: scratch a boy, you get his mother.

18   Peggy just fell off the sofa.

19   In college, I worked for awhile for Eric Bentley, who was a playwright and the translator of Bertolt Brecht's plays. He taught at Columbia but resigned in solidarity with the student protests in 1968. I got the job through a campus listing.

20   I am not sure I can convey my parents' joy when sometime in the 80s they received passports that, in place of any one country, said European Union, in three languages.

21   Bentley was old and famous, and he had me do paperwork. Soon he started showing me Polaroids of black hustlers he sometimes brought home.

22   One I will never forget because he had a white athletic sock hanging over his cock while he smiled at the camera.

23   Another time with Camille, we had to go through her hair with a nit comb and wash everything in hot water because she picked up head lice at summer camp.

24   And then they came back.

25   Her scalp was so irritated, she cried from the combing. I offered to stop and she said no, do it.

xxxiv

I once had sex with a prostitute in Kevin Killian   1
and Dodie Bellamy's apartment.

He only told me he was a prostitute after we   2
had sex. I met him in a club in San Francisco;
he was in a band that had just played, called the
Popstitutes. Apparently everyone in the band was
a prostitute.

Sometimes people's comments on my random   3
things are better than my random things.

I had just been told by an ex that I had scabies, and   4
had to go to a clinic to get the right soap to kill
them. I washed all the sheets and told Kevin and
Dodie not to worry, but I could tell they were a
little worried. This wasn't the first time I ever stayed
with them, but it might have been the second.

I was much younger then.   5

The video card on my laptop is giving out and   6
just now the corner of the page I'm writing lifted
or blacked out and then came back again.

I think during this same visit Dodie and Eileen   7
Myles, who was staying there too, had a terrible
screaming fight, which both of them wrote about
later.

Actually the club where the Popstitutes were   8
playing might have been called the Klubstitute.

A while ago I saw a video on YouTube of an   9
elephant painting itself, or painting another
elephant.

There are a lot of videos like this, with people   10
staring on in amazement.

11　I think it's about us, not the elephants. Our pleasure at seeing the elephants reflecting on themselves is really about our desire to see ourselves reflected in everything we see.

12　Oh, the foolish cult of Matthew Barney.

13　It seems I'm about a third of the way through now. It doesn't feel any definite way though. I'm still just writing sentences.

14　I try never to know what's coming next.

15　There are in Yiddish two words that mark an important distinction that exists in no other language: the *schlemeil* and the *schlamazel*. Two kinds of unlucky or klutzy people, but in the spilling of a bowl of soup, the *schlemeil* will inevitably be the one who spills it, and the *schlamazel* is the one who gets the soup spilled on him.

16　No one I know will confess to reading or liking a self-help book, but I actually love *The Power of Now*.

17　I remember once suddenly noticing the backs of people's heads, their hair, in a classroom or a theater.

18　It might have been after getting glasses or contact lenses.

19　Suddenly every hair was visible, a whole head of hair, one by one. And lots of heads, a whole room of heads of hair.

20　Another in that line of recognitions was when I first saw Jean Dunning's photographs of women's hair, shot so you couldn't tell if it was from the back, or the front with the hair combed forward

You looked at it and thought, wow, every hair counts. 21

The thing about eyes that interests me is that they both see and are looked at, often intensely. 22

I remember my mother once said to me: we're not German, we're European. 23

You reach a certain point in your life and you look back, and if you do not find forgiveness, you come up with a new concept of need. Your parent, your ex, or the driver of the car that hit you wasn't doing anything but what they needed to do at that time. 24

So you kind of put need in the place of either intention or chance. 25

XXXV

I think it's funny how everyone thinks Colombia is a university, and Cali stands for California. 1

Who knew there was so much need in the world? 2

Russel Swensen's mother thinks he's wrong, in the existential sense, and my mother thought I was right. Almost as if my father was wrong and I was right. 3

Right for being gay, right for being sensitive, right for being smart. 4

It's hard to be right so much. Maybe not as hard as being wrong, but think about it. 5

In a core way, I think these lists are really about the sentence. 6

We read in the newspaper today that 45% of the world's wealth has been destroyed in the last year. 7

8   I thought that matter could not disappear, only be transformed. So isn't someone sitting there with all that money?

9   Unless the lesson of it all is that money is not real, and I'm not sure I'm ready to believe that.

10   The Leafy Sea Dragon is a seahorse that looks like seaweed. We love these weird creatures. The sea cucumber, or the walking stick, things that seem both animal and vegetable at the same time.

11   If something's not random, it can still be a fragment.

12   Can you consider this a sort of atomized writing? Atomic. Aphoristic. Like Nietzsche, not in its gravity, but its style.

13   Am I the only one who is surprised that spell check doesn't know how to spell Nietzsche?

14   I should confess that I didn't actually read *The Power of Now*. I listened to it on tape. I play it in my car when I am low, really low. I play it again and again.

15   I keep thinking that at key points, like a third of the way through, I need a plot point, like describing Kathy Acker's death.

16   And I'm holding back my ace, my mother's death two years later.

17   I have stared death in the face, and is it wrong to say I found it beautiful?

18   My aunt Amanda, when I was young, once told me she had failed my uncle, her husband George. He was old enough to be her father and as his health and mind started to decline, she had put him in a nursing home, where he died alone.

If this writing isn't random, could you say it's randomesque? 19

It is only when you fail someone, she said, utterly and miserably, that you are finally free. 20

Things like this, when you hear them at the right time, can start doors swinging in your mind that never stop. Whole buildings lose their foundations. 21

Peggy is biting her nails. 22

My aunt was prone to grand, mystical, and existential pronouncements. 23

There is a new meme going around, the fuckit list. It's a list of things you don't care if you ever do or see, etc., in your life. 24

It's a play on the bucket list, which begins with the premise that you have only a year to live, and is the list of things you'd want to do, see, etc., before you die. See the Taj Mahal, go on a game show, etc. 25

xxxvi

Certain words, like truncheon or cudgel, really express something about human nature. 1

Or bludgeon. All those old Anglo-Saxon words like root or blood. Ugh. They're not logical or easy to trace, like the word unification, or bicameralism. 2

The deaths in my childhood were like ellipses instead of full stops. My parents just stopped talking about people. 3

My father's father, Eberhard, fell over drunk one night and died of an aneurysm. His death got mentioned a few weeks later, just an aside. 4

5   Even my grandmother, who did die a sort of elliptical death, at 100, almost senile, in a nursing home. It took a few weeks there, too.

6   Of all the times I've talked to people next to me on flights, the only friend I made that way was Marina LaPalma.

7   A lot of Anglo-Saxon words are body words: the guts.

8   And the ones from Latin are the head words, like cogitate, or implication.

9   One night when I was living at the beach with my boyfriend, we all stood outside waiting for a tsunami.

10   There had been an earthquake offshore in Alaska and the news said a wave was coming, so we stood on a hill about 75 feet above the beach.

11   I love to think about words.

12   The tsunami never came, and when the people dwindled I noticed a guy standing near me who had a sort of erection in his pants and kept looking at me. He was very nice looking.

13   Eventually we started talking and we ended up having sex nearby in an empty house that was being renovated.

14   My nails have been bitten down in the last week. I must be anxious.

15   *The Wizard of Oz* is such an American story.

16   It's a dream of a parallel world, or a dream on the power of wishes, and a nostalgia for a home that never was.

I remember marigolds, that hot orange color, that smell.

17

It was the same color as the tracks to my Hot Wheels set, which I used to run through the marigolds.

18

What's great about eccentric museums like the Gardner in Boston is that they remind us how much art has been about rich people and their quirks—before they get smoothed out by an army of professionals.

19

When I was seduced during a performance of *Einstein on the Beach*, the guy started by first placing his leg against mine. I let it stay there.

20

Then after a while our hands touched. And I let mine stay there.

21

I remember how hot our fingers felt. Then after a long time, really, we were basically holding hands.

22

I think it's what made *Einstein* such a great theatrical experience for me. After all, it doesn't really have a plot, and this way it did.

23

The best untranslatable German word I know is *Weltschmerz*, not *Zeitgeist*, which is overused. *Weltschmerz* is a feeling of melancholy and world-weariness, a kind of world-ache.

24

A lot of the best seductions move slowly and happen while something else is going on.

25

xxxvii

At some point, if you keep listing random things about yourself, people will start to have ideas about you.

1

2   I've been trying to distract you by telling you either racy sex stories or melancholic family stories.

3   All the stuff people crave.

4   Colin Dickey says there is a good fruit-theft scene in *Les Misérables* too.

5   Eberhard Viegener, my grandfather, was the great artist of our family. He was a sort of dead father ghost; he was a bad father but he couldn't help it. He was a philanderer, sort of, and a drunk. But his paintings were great.

6   I'm saying things here I would never say to my father.

7   During the War they took in a refugee, Annemarie, whose father was a famous communist who died in a concentration camp. Annemarie became Eberhard's mistress and appeared in a series of paintings as a sort of black angel figure.

8   My father and his siblings called Annemarie *die Schlange*, the snake, which is also the root for the Yiddish word *schlong*, or penis.

9   Someone gave me a one-way mirror when I was about nine, and I spent many weeks playing with it. I wanted to construct a sort of infinite light box of mirrors on five sides with a one-way mirror on the sixth. I thought I could point it at the sky and collect sunlight until it melted the box, or melted me.

10   After the War my grandfather, grandmother, and Annemarie lived together for nearly a decade. Annemarie had a son by Eberhard and my grandmother sent my father a picture of his half brother, saying he was sweet. She signed it "your

little mother," in German. She called herself
"little mother."

I guess that is not a heartwarming story, but I see   11
some humor in it.

Car horns, just now, on the street below.   12

True, truer, and truest, all the meat around truth,   13
which people seem to think they are cutting to
get "close to the bone," all the stuff of truthiness.

Quotation marks in German are like »this« and in   14
French like «this».

The Germans call them »little goose feet.«   15

I'm wondering if this reflects anything about each   16
culture. Like that the French need to contain things
and the Germans to prop them up with little feet.

The French call them *«guillemets»* or williamses,   17
after the guy, William, who made the first ones.

There's a story in my family about my   18
grandmother as a little girl. Her family was friends
with Johannes Brahms, who famously liked little
girls very much. So every time he came over they
would plop my grandmother on his lap, just like
that, and she grew to like it, quite a bit indeed.

Maybe all this is about a certain streak of   19
perversity that skipped from my grandparents to
me and spared my parents.

There's a new thing going around Facebook   20
where you Google "unfortunately [your name],"
and then collect the top ten results into a poem.

Mine is all about unlucky soccer players and   21
mishaps on vacations.

22   My father didn't really want to be a jewelry designer. He wanted to be an architect.

23   Are memes now the only way people can say new things about themselves?

24   Too much miming in the memes, and too little me.

25   "Unfortunately, Matias, you just weren't able to win."

xxxviii

1   It occurs to me that what I've been treating as a bad cold, might really be an allergy.

2   I never had allergies as a child, so if I do have one I'm not sure what it feels like, and some part of me thinks it's not possible to suddenly have an allergy when you didn't before.

3   This is a rather German sentiment. My father did not believe in allergies, saying that allergies were just a lack of willpower.

4   I like mustard, but I don't really love it. It is the food that will last the longest in my refrigerator. I have a jar of violet mustard from France that must be 15 years old. It's made with real violets by monks in a monastery.

5   It's still good!

6   Sometimes I hit the wrong key and it comes OUT IN ALL CAPS. I then go back and delete because caps are supposed to be rude, as if you're shouting.

7   Nothing is like a seductive student.

It is a very German idea: that so much is in our minds. This has a real downside, but it's also what made things like psychoanalysis possible. 8

The only souvenirs I usually bring home from trips are rocks. 9

I like that they are all different but all the same. 10

Also when I'm dead there will be less to take care of. Someone will just sweep up the rocks and throw them in the garden. 11

Like my father, I am not ticklish. Unless you catch me by surprise. But like him, I learned to master the tickle impulse through willpower. 12

In the mirror today: some grey hair. 13

I don't steal other people's random things, but I do get inspired by them. I read about tickling on one of my ex-student's lists. 14

Over time all the rocks in my garden will get covered and mashed together by tremendous geological powers, and one day a scientist from another planet will uncover them and notice how all these rocks found all over the world were also found together in one spot. And what will it mean? 15

We had a tremendous number of houseplants when I was growing up, over three hundred. 16

When I first heard Patti Smith sing "Jesus died for somebody's sins but not mine," I was all, "not mine either!" 17

I have been sleeping in my guest room for years now. It just feels right. Plus my bedroom gets morning sun, and who wants that? 18

19 And another thing: automatic deposits.

20 For years my paycheck from CalArts has arrived invisibly, and I never think about it. Sometimes I forget what I get paid for. The checking account just automatically seems to refill.

21 Kate McAnergney asked me today if I was reaching some kind of list-induced *samadhi*—a state of intense concentration achieved through meditation. In Hindu yoga this is regarded as the final stage at which union with the divine is reached before or at death.

22 It's also the word for a funerary monument.

23 That's interesting. For the most part I think all graves are ugly.

24 *Samadhi*'s etymology comes from *sam* (together or integrated), *a* (towards), and *dha* (to get, to hold). So the result would be to acquire integration or wholeness, or truth. No more fragments, I guess.

25 I heard on the radio tonight a jobless person saying what it was like when the automatic deposits stop. It felt like a stab in the gut.

xxxix

1 I've flown alone so often, it seems strange to me to travel with another person. The minute I walk onto an airplane I become a kind of worm.

2 My favorite kind of flight is an unconscious flight.

3 There are a few things you could say about where cheese comes from.

4 Cheese comes from cows; cheese comes from a word in Old English; cheese comes from the need to preserve fresh milk.

There's something I like about this, versus, let's say, a lot of art. 5

Here is a chair, here is a picture of a chair, here is a definition of a chair, etc. 6

Once I met Lance Loud, the gay teenage son from the first reality show, on public television, in the 1970s. *American Family*. In one season he came out to his parents, moved to NY, and became a musician and a club kid. 7

I met him in a club in LA and he picked me up, flipped my legs over his shoulders, and let me dangle upside down. 8

Hello, world! 9

I'm on my way to Cali, Colombia. I'm trying not to have any ideas about it before I get there. I'm trying to arrive without ideas, only eyes. 10

I am not sure at this time that I would be inclined to write anything at all long. I'm so in the rhythm of little things. Sentences. 11

For us it is so normal to see clouds from above, and inside. 12

When my mother was in a coma and dying, I took a plane to NY, and for the first time, I talked on one of those in-flight telephones. 13

It cost about $10 a minute and I didn't care. My mother was dying. 14

I called my two cousins, Bettina and Susana. I told them everything I knew, which wasn't much. 15

It felt like if I could talk from the sky, then surely my mother could survive. 16

17   Sianne Ngai mentioned in a note that she too had become allergy prone, which I mistook for allegory prone. I certainly have a tendency toward allegory.

18   An allegory is a sort of extended metaphor, often narrative, telling one story in terms of another, indirectly related one.

19   The allergy is an "other energy," and Germans were the first to use the word. And allegory is "other speaking," a hidden meaning buried inside a story.

20   We are flying into the darkest purple storm clouds, fierce angry mushroom clouds with lightning coming out sideways toward us. The whole plane shakes, and I cannot believe the wings can flex like this and not break off.

21   I think very few things can be told directly, so the indirect route is usually the only one possible.

22   Animal videos on the airplane monitors keep people laughing. Dogs torturing cats, cats stalking people and then unfurling yards of toilet paper as if possessed.

23   To me these animal videos have some relation to the cute, miniaturized meals we are served on airplanes.

24   Out the window I see tropical torpor, the setting sun, the equatorial climate, and what seem to me to be the somatic zones. Somatic means "of the body," and in the 19th century the British decided, since it was too hot for them to think there, tropical climates favored feelings and the senses.

25   We're almost here and I can't wait to stop thinking.

xl

I had a new fruit today from a street vendor in Cali. It's called a *chontaduro*, it comes from a palm tree and is supposed to be an aphrodisiac. It tastes kind of like a roasted chestnut and is served with salt.

1

Sometimes my mother would call upon the golem. Usually when there was something impossible to get done, the golem would save us.

2

It was kind of my mother, who wanted to be Jewish, rather than my father, who was.

3

We're staying in an artist's residency called Lugar a Dudas, or place of doubt.

4

For all the echoes of doubt, everyone is extremely warm and friendly.

5

There is nothing luckier than to be interested in things, interested in your own life.

6

Sometimes on airplanes I just pretend to have fastened my seat belt.

7

Think about those TV game shows in which, when you are stumped, you get one chance to call a friend.

8

In Germany, a health food store is called a *Reformhaus*.

9

I wear ear plugs to sleep here, because there is a club next door that plays loud American music into the night.

10

There is something about good ear plugs that really cuts you off from the world, and makes you more of a worm.

11

12   I found out about the best ear plugs from David Wright, who cannot sleep without them, but I'm afraid to wear them every night. What if I become dependant and can never sleep without them?

13   I walked into a smell memory here, a sort of sweet, burnt rubber odor that reminds me of the Metro in Paris.

14   About ten years ago I drove to Las Vegas in the middle of the summer with David Burns. It was over 110 degrees every day, and we were in his Ford Taurus station wagon with broken air conditioning.

15   It is not possible to describe the feeling, other than to say at some point you don't notice the heat anymore.

16   I love those 90s Ford Taurus station wagons. They look like killer whales, white bodies with big swooping black windows. Cartoon killer whales swimming backwards.

17   I remember when I was a kid and the local teen pervert, who was maybe four years older than the rest of us, would lurk in a park waiting to catch us.

18   Once I walked in on him playing with his penis. He was sitting on the ground with his white briefs pulled over his head and his eyes looking out where each leg should be.

19   He asked me if I wanted to touch it, and I laughed and ran away.

20   For a few years after 9/11, passengers started applauding after their planes landed, but now I notice it doesn't happen any more.

The only thing stranger than calling a part of your 21
body "it" is to call it by another person's name.
Your Peter. Your Dick.

After my mother died, she wanted to be cremated. 22
We all agreed that after you were dead, it didn't
matter. The body is not the person, and the
ashes are really not the person. In fact we kept
forgetting to scatter them.

Her ashes were in my father's house for four years, 23
until he sold it to move away. When he and my
brother were packing his things, they decided to
scatter her ashes in the woods without telling or
asking me.

Now, I think it does matter what happens to the 24
ashes.

What if the Euro collapses? 25

xli

There are little android mushrooms growing from 1
the cracks of the patio by our door.

All the rooms at Lugar a Dudas are open in some 2
way, from the courtyard surrounded by the rooms
to the living room which has an open ceiling with
cloth awnings pulled open all day.

In California we like to pretend we are tropical, 3
but we are not.

The Cali River is small and rust-colored, and it 4
bubbles with storm water from the mountains.

Wink is a great English word, not onomatopoeic 5
but it ought to be. You can imagine eyelids
making that sound. In Spanish winks are *guiños*.

6   How difficult it is to be in one place at a time. Marcella Sinclair, an Argentine artist in residency here, said this today as we talked about places we'd been and those to which we want to go.

7   The first thing they proudly showed us today in Nashira, the women's eco-village, was the new composting toilet that keeps the urine separated from the shit. They have to keep it locked because the children still don't understand the system.

8   Before I left LA I had hearts of palm with Susan Silton, and yesterday on the menu I saw *corazones del pollo*, chicken hearts.

9   While listening to an artist's presentation I could half follow in Spanish, I checked my email on my iPhone wedged between my legs like a rectangular, flat-screen phallus.

10   A group of us went to the coast south of San Francisco to scatter Kathy Acker's ashes. But her psychic, a giddy man whose name I forgot, grabbed the ashes and made a run for the ocean, shrieking, "You're free Kathy, you're free!"

11   Today I ate *uchuva*, or cape gooseberries. They are like sweet yellow tomatillos surrounded by papery husks.

12   Amy Scholder and I were nearest and the others urged us to chase him from the cliff above the beach. But Kathy's ashes flew into the ocean with the shrieking psychic who none of us liked.

13   The only thing I could think was that you're born into this world at the hands of people who don't know who you are, which is most likely how you will leave it.

14   I rented a Yugo once. It was a ridiculous little car.

Sometimes a person wearing earplugs thinks that   15
no one else hears what they can't hear.

Actually the music isn't keeping me awake, it's the   16
bass rhythm from the club next door. And there's
a loud wedding on the opposite side.

I took ecstasy once with an ex-boyfriend at Glen   17
Ivy Hot Springs. I suddenly found fat people
extremely beautiful, with lavish and generous
bodies.

Try to explain to a Colombian the difference   18
between Americans and Canadians.

In paleontology, the fossils indicate that parrots   19
once flew wild over what is now Norway and
Denmark.

This reminds me of the line "Mrs. Anderson's   20
Swedish baby / Might well have been German or
Spanish, / But that things go round and again go
round / Has rather a classical sound."

That Wallace Stevens poem is supposed to be   21
about the question of paternity, but I thought it
was more about randomness, or chance.

I once walked through a pet cemetery in the   22
desert with Kathy, and the best grave read: "Every
little breeze seems to whisper Critter."

One of Kathy's favorite books was *Valley of the*   23
Dolls, which is one of my favorite movies. I often
sang the theme song to myself as a kid.

I saw the expression to give something "wide   24
berth" in print, and I realized for a long time I
somehow mingled berth with birth.

25   It's one of those colloquial expressions you think
     are entirely natural until you examine them, like
     the idea of "taking something on."

xlii

1   When I can't sleep, I think of my dog Peggy
     sleeping. I think of her limp body and her
     breathing.

2   For years before this, I thought of all my friends
     in Silver Lake. I'd picture where they lived, streets
     near my street, their houses, their bedrooms, their
     beds. I'd think of them sleeping, as if they led the
     way and I could follow them.

3   Soon after Kathy died in Tijuana, I went to Banff,
     Canada for an artist's residency. I went from
     warm to cold, from Mexican nurses to glaciers,
     and from the dying to the athletic.

4   I arrived on the winter solstice, and the days were
     very short.

5   Sylvère Lotringer was there, and a few times we
     went to the hot springs. Every morning we took
     walks in the snow.

6   It was like *The Magic Mountain*.

7   When we arrived at Nashira yesterday, the
     members were in a meeting because of an
     opportunity for a group to be sent to work in
     Spain—but only men.

8   Nashira is the women's eco-village, run by women
     from the Asociación Mujeres Cabeza de Familia,
     an association of women who head families.

9   A third of Colombian households are run by
     women; three quarters of these households,

whose women are the main source of income, are
below the poverty line.

Sometimes I would ask Andy to fall asleep first so   10
I could follow him there, and it worked.

The women at Nashira were choosing which of   11
their brothers, sons, and a few husbands, to send
abroad to work. We could hear them discussing
who they could spare and who the village needed
most.

The grenadilla is like a passionfruit only milder,   12
with a slight floral sweetness. The black seeds are
in a light grey gel, and it looks almost like caviar.

I saw a man juggling onions in the street.   13

It's raining outside, a warm gentle rain. You could   14
sit naked in the courtyard and enjoy it.

People's sense of what is sweet is variable. A   15
woman told us yesterday that bananas are too
sweet.

As we were mapping fruit trees in the   16
neighborhood of Miraflores, a man leaned out
the window and told us to put our cameras in our
bags. Then a nasty-looking Colombian punk boy
passed us and sneered, and when he was about
50 feet beyond us he yelled (in English), "People
who want to change the world are faggots."

What if we all made decisions according to what   17
was best for the village?

I have all these frequent flyer miles I've never   18
used. Once I used them to take an ex to Europe
and that ended poorly.

Since then I save them for a rainy day.   19

20   The word for equal in Spanish is *igual*, which I remember from *égal* in French, which was easy for me to remember because in German it is *egal*.

21   Sleep is so hard to get when you don't have it, so hard to lose when you have too much.

22   When I was a kid I read about the *Lamed Vavniks*, 36 righteous people on whom the world depends—but we don't know who they are. They could be the bus driver, or anyone.

23   I worry sometimes I'm not random enough.

24   Now it's pouring rain outside.

25   You'd think that travel would increase the randomness of anyone's life, but in a way everything that happens is connected by space and time.

xliii

1   We found the town of Ciénaga, where the banana massacre took place in 1928.

2   What did the striking banana workers want?

3   To work six, not seven days, for only eight hours, with health care, earning wages not company vouchers. And they wanted toilets.

4   I had *pan de yuca,* yucca bread, which is crunchy outside and very gooey inside.

5   The banana strike and the massacre happened 80 years ago, a decade after the Communist revolution.

6   Julia tells us that cheap shoes from Cali last forever, unless you take them out of the city, where they immediately fall apart.

I am loving my collaborators. 7

Talking to Julia, who has never been to the 8
US, gives me insight into what it means to be
American. We have an unbounded quality, the
illusion that basically it doesn't matter where you
are from, who your family is.

One of my students, Vandy Martin, gave me her 9
fat Webster's dictionary when she graduated. She
wrote in a note that she would no longer need
such an old-fashioned thing.

For several hours we found ourselves telling Julia 10
stories of immigrants to the US.

Austin is better at spotting fruit trees than I am. 11

We flew from Cali to Barranquilla in a Fokker. 12

The people in the eco-village association are the 13
same people as, or the descendants of, the banana
workers in Ciénaga.

Some of us are free and some of us are slaves. 14

I dramatically lost grasp of what Spanish I did 15
have when I was twenty, and decided I had to
learn Italian, because, you know, it is so musical.
Not understanding that of all the romance
languages, Spanish is the most vital, the one most
about the future.

There was a bird caught in the airport terminal 16
in Cali, and a bat in the terminal in Barranquilla.

Philosophy and the philosophy of language, it's 17
hard to separate them, isn't it?

South America is more a continent of the future 18
than Europe, the continent of the past.

19   I read today that Nashira, the women's eco-village, is from the Arabic word for bearer of good news. It's the name of a star 139 light years away.

20   I have a head full of trivia. Rather like Susan Sontag, who undeniably had some good trivia.

21   I think Sontag was a good reader, not a great thinker. And definitely not a fiction writer.

22   What does it mean to be a communist anymore?

23   By listing random things, I sometimes feel I'm dismantling my mind rather than adding anything to it.

24   One of the most damning things is to just flatter people's intelligence.

25   This may become a book that exhausts all my ideas in their most telegraphic or epigrammatic form and leaves me broken and exhausted.

xliv

1   All the street dogs we have seen in Colombia are incredibly cute. I have a theory about this. The dogs that survive on the street are invariably the cute ones, the ones people feed. The ugly dogs die.

2   This is not unlike fruit. Often the cute fruit survives and the ugly fruit perishes. This leads to misfortune, like Red Delicious apples, which are handsome but taste awful.

3   We read three books and countless articles on the history of the banana, all pretty much saying the same thing. But everything people here told us about the banana massacre is different, which makes us wonder if any of the authors actually came here.

It's interesting that David, who often reads bird 4
signs, did not see either of the birds in the two
airport terminals the other day.

I spent the day in bed with food poisoning in a 5
hotel room overlooking the big blue Caribbean,
freezing under the blankets while it was 108°
outside.

Two historians in Ciénaga told us the first, 6
and last, time anyone from elsewhere came to
interview them was the BBC thirty years ago. It
was the fifty-year anniversary of the *masacre de las
bananeras*.

Is it only from my perspective as a fruit person 7
that this history is important?

Nikki once gave me a beautiful painted egg that 8
said, "Trenton makes, the world takes," the slogan
of Trenton, NJ.

One of the first modern multinational 9
corporations develops a new form of monopoly
capitalism, dominating the global trade in
bananas. And the workers, *bananeros*, are killed
over something as ordinary and simple as fruit?
No one agrees how many *bananeros* were killed.
It could be eight, or fifty. Some say six or eight
hundred. Others have said up to three thousand.

Remember carbon paper? 10

Everything here takes three times longer than it 11
should. Don't be surprised.

People have often started drawing diagrams for 12
us, and then finished them on the table itself, so
when we leave them, we actually only have half
the directions.

13   We saw a man sleeping under a park bench yesterday, which reminded me of drug addicts in New York. One place I lived in had so many heroin addicts passed out in the building, on the steps, etc., that you wouldn't even stop to see if they were dead.

14   And the United Fruit Company, how it echoes the name United States.

15   Having visited Santa Marta and Ciénaga, I think that García Márquez pretty much writes realism.

16   What is beautiful about a Latin culture is how people stop everything just to talk to us.

17   The primacy of human contact.

18   What makes a great narrative?

19   Comprehensible terms.

20   Gravity.

21   And an enduring need for a thing to be told. Even when the "truth" is hard to isolate, like the numbers of bodies, or the actual locations.

22   This is the first time I have needed an umbrella in the sun.

23   Colombia is named after Christopher Columbus. America after Amerigo Vespucci. And "discovery" as a concept, aren't things like this enough to make you suspicious of it?

24   As much as "know," as in, "I know about the banana."

25   One of my childhood friends had the album *101 Musical Masterpieces*. Only it wasn't all

the masterpieces, just bits of them. Her father would drop the needle on the record, and quiz her brother. It was usually something like the Tchaikovsky symphony they turned into the song "Tonight We Love."

xlv

In Santa Marta and Ciénaga we saw three pigs crossing the road, more than two dozen donkeys, about a hundred men with machetes, and uncountable soldiers with machine guns.   1

Most American fiction is trivial. It's either self-reflexive or exhausted. Or it's all: pay attention to me!   2

There is something great about getting really sick, going down, way down, so just keeping still in bed is an achievement.   3

And then the ride up, the world coming back to life, words coming back, smells, being able to think and see.   4

How can I tell you what it was like, to travel this far and finally be on a big green banana plantation, a *bananera*, the source of the most popular fruit in the world?   5

There is something random about getting sick.   6

I made Julia laugh by saying a group of new hotels looks like Gringolandia.   7

In Colombia there is a chain of coffee places called Juan Valdez. Looking at its logo, I recognized Juan from TV advertisements when I was a kid.   8

He was called *el exigente*, the demanding one. He was a tough coffee taster traveling to plantations   9 in remote places, and he would demonstrate the quality of Colombian coffee by haughtily rejecting a farmer's coffee. At the end, he finally finds one he likes and the whole village cheers.

10 Words in Spanish used in my family: *liquadora, asado, bichos,* and *simpático.*

11 In David's family I have often noticed that they are crankier with each other than with anyone else they know.

12 Me and Argentina: I always wanted to go back, since I was 13, when my uncle who had a cattle ranch told me I should come for a summer to learn to properly ride a horse.

13 And this beautiful language.

14 My mother was a photographer.

15 After I was eighteen, I was forbidden to visit Argentina because my family was convinced I would be kidnapped for not performing Argentine military service.

16 In filming the *bananeros,* and talking to them, I was overcome sometimes with feeling, I guess something like love.

17 My parents always idealized workers, especially skilled workers: carpenters, farmers, people who worked with their hands. I found this terribly embarrassing.

18 But maybe it's an antidote to the boring world around us, to kitsch, celebrity, and the culture of genius.

19 I've never done any kind of repetitive work.

Grading papers is as close as I've come, or making lists. 20

I like chopping vegetables, but after a while I lose patience with it. 21

Whenever we saw a dead animal by the side of the road, my mother used to pull over. She told us it was almost the only time you could see a truly wild animal up close. 22

I do have repetitive habits, like reading, analyzing, and what could be more repetitive than sleeping? 23

I remember seeing a dead stray dog rotting by the side of the road in Tijuana, while Kathy was dying in a hospital nearby. 24

People didn't walk around it; they just stepped over it. It was covered in flies. 25

xlvi

My pillow is gone! 1

Why is utopianism so uncool with so many people I know? 2

You know that if men menstruated, the world would be run by a lunar calendar. 3

My favorite mistake in English that my mother made was when arriving in someone's house, she would occasionally exclaim how "homely" it was! 4

Sometimes when salesmen knocked on the door, my friend Marc Weisman's mother would say, "Please go away, I am not interesting." 5

I just looked in the mirror and I look like me again. 6

7   Today I have more than 25 things, so I will save some.

8   Four years ago, we could not have come to Santa Marta and Ciénaga because they were being torn apart by paramilitaries and guerrillas.

9   Chris Kraus once told me that Sylvère Lotringer and I were the only two men she knew who did not see Kathy Acker as monstrous.

10 I remember visiting the Greek island of Delos, filled with marble phalluses. Many of them had been chopped off at the stem, so to speak.

11 I envy Austin, his capacity to fall asleep anywhere at any time. This would make my life much easier.

12 What about men who cup their balls and call them the family jewels?

13 Or men who name their penises?

14 More rain. I will probably always see weather as a New Yorker; I spent my "formative years" where weather was something you struggled against.

15 Few things are as embarrassing as your own mother.

16 I had sex in a bathroom at UCLA during the Rodney King riots. It was with an architecture student. We even talked about it: having sex while the city burned.

17 For a long time, I believed in ancient astronauts.

18 I've heard stories about strangers having sex in bomb shelters during the War.

19 I remember when people got dressed up to travel. When I was a kid we had special traveling outfits.

Pompeii is filled with phallic statues.   20

When I was a kid, my mother's aunt would come   21
visit us every year from Germany. The first few
times she wore a wool jacket and skirt, stuffed
inside like a sausage.

In a hot climate, if you're not peeing, you're not   22
drinking enough.

My mother's aunt was kind of dowdy, and she   23
never looked as good as when she traveled.

By the end of the 80s things had changed, and   24
she arrived in rumpled sweat suits.

What about when they paint fig leaves over classic   25
nude paintings?

xlvii

What we did not find at Nashira was the *jejé*, a local   1
fly whose sting is like a badly inserted hypodermic
needle, followed by spurting blood and intense
pain. I almost wish we did find one, so terrible an
insect, with a name that sounds like laughter.

The 1970s was the most liberal time I ever lived   2
through. It had an openness, a sense of imminent
social change.

All of this disappeared immediately in the 1980s,   3
a cynical, hard decade.

I am very frustrated with this format. The things   4
I've been thinking don't fit. This is not a space for
complex thoughts.

We got almost nothing done on our last day at   5
Nashira, the women's eco-village. We were trying
to shoot a video with the kids. Nothing worked

out as we planned and we realized that we hardly spoke the same language, and I do not mean English and Spanish.

6   Last week we went to a beautiful school in Cali called Colegio Ideas to videotape the students eating fruit.

7   We loved Ideas. It's the kind of school you wish you went to. No walls, animals roaming around, teachers hugging students all the time.

8   After seeing the "danger / guns" sign on the banana plantation, we asked the watchman if bananas and guns always went together. Yes, he said, always.

9   This has been more like a diary than a list during my trip to Colombia.

10   It's like my memories of the present. But the present seems less random for some reason than other random things.

11   Maybe because these things are linked by the concept of Cali, or Colombia, or here and now.

12   Today I woke up and I felt like a camera, just a mechanical register of things.

13   There is a dream of Latin America that I recognize here and there, and in the way my parents talked about it. I see it in the native handicrafts or weavings people love so much here. It is a dream of a vital indigenous tradition with European values.

14   I don't think I need to add a comment on idealism and politics.

15   The first moving pictures were either flip books or illustrated scrolls. It depends on what you think moving means.

Felt and left have the same letters. As do face and   16
café. But is this meaningful?

I felt left.   17

When we arrived at the Ideas school, we were   18
led to a little wooded clearing to eat the lunch
we brought with us. In the bushes at the end of
the clearing, two teenagers were rolling around
making out.

The teacher asked them what was going on. They   19
just got up and walked away, their pants covered
in mud.

The weirdest term for bathroom I've found is   20
WC, water closet. You see it in France more than
in England.

I worry that I'm repeating myself. Is that a sign of   21
randomness, or its opposite?

Lavatory is pretty odd too, though I guess people   22
do wash themselves in bathrooms.

The curriculum at the Ideas school is organized   23
by the categories of air, earth, water, and fire.

I wonder if they learn history or math.   24

As we passed a heap of watermelon-sized rocks,   25
the teacher told me they were their ancestor
stones. Often they are carried to the fire to sit
with the students, and then carried back.

xlviii

I chewed coca leaves twice in Colombia.   1

Coca grows all over and it is said that activists   2
scatter the seeds everywhere in protest of both the

global control and the political manipulation of the coca plant.

3   At the Ideas school they believe in elves and fairies. They also believe that their students are mostly elves and fairies. The boys are elves and the girls are fairies.

4   My mother needed coffee so badly, she would drink a cup of instant coffee in the morning to wake up enough to make real coffee.

5   One of the boys at Ideas told me that they were about to have a corn dance in which they gathered all the corn into a huge heap, then set it on fire and stayed up all night dancing around it.

6   Doesn't every son want to make a movie whose star is his mother?

7   When we arrived they were having a ritual dance to bid farewell to the teachers-in-training from Bogotá, who had come to learn about new ideas in pedagogy.

8   I should mention that Ideas is a private school and all the children have white teeth and wealthy families.

9   I love women with deep voices. Argentina has many; lots of Latin countries do. It's so sexy.

10 In its ideal form, Nashira, the women's eco-village, represents something Christine Wertheim and I have always talked about: forms of culture that have a real effect, like teaching in prisons, etc. It's idealistic in every way, and utopian in ways that are so unfashionable among the people I know. People prefer their utopias to be speculative, or doomed.

When I was about eleven years old, my best friend   11
Seth and I started what we called "collecting
license plates." We would walk to the nearest
main street, sit down on the curb, and list all the
states we found.

At first it was easy but it became harder and   12
harder. You don't find cars from Montana or
Oregon or Alaska in New York.

There is so much to be said about native plants   13
and the desires of the colonizers. Also the needs
of the colonized.

For several weeks, all I did when I rode in cars   14
or buses was look at license plates. Anyone who
has ever done something like this can tell you
how hard it is to stop, once you do it without
thinking. I still catch myself looking toward what
you could call the belly button of the car, and
then I stop myself.

Sometimes reality interferes with things, like   15
when you are on a trip but still try to make a list of
random things. Or not reality—when experience
takes precedence over thought, which is what
randomizes things more than anything else.

Experience is both contingent and random.   16

Coca and guns have gone together ever since the   17
Europeans arrived in South America.

Counting is such a human thing. No one counts   18
but us. Nothing counts but us.

In Colombia there is a drug they use to rob or rape   19
people. *Burundanga* is from the bark of a native
tree and, slipped into your drink, it will make you
lose all willpower and say yes to anything people
ask.

20 Julia told us that men used to blow the powder at women on the bus, and for a few years all the women covered their faces from the nose down with magazines or newspapers.

21 A few hours later you wake up in the jungle with no wallet, jewelry or cell phones. And often they even take your shoes.

22 Seth and I also collected coins. The only thing I remember about it was that the one coin everyone wanted most was the 1909 SVDB Lincoln penny. The designer's initials, VDB, were only on the coin for a few days. Then the mint took them off and melted down all those pennies, except a handful.

23 It is easier to manipulate crowds of people with fear than with desire.

24 Like the anthrax epidemic.

25 What is chewing coca leaves like? It has sort of a grassy wintergreen quality, and then your mouth feels numb. Overall, it resembles a visit to the dentist.

xlix

1 The night before we left Cali, Leandra, a local artist, made us lulo jam with psychedelic mushrooms.

2 If it wasn't the night before we were leaving, we would have eaten more of it.

3 Cheryl Klein mentioned something about the power of collecting nonmaterial things.

4 Yes, I think it is a cousin of things like making a list of who you would sleep with in a room if you

had to chose one person, and then another—a list in declining order.

Collecting is a human thing.   5

The place we stayed in Cali was next door to a   6
rock club with a Colombian band playing mostly covers of American rock songs. The stage was on the other side of our wall, with really loud music most nights until 3 a.m.

In retrospect, I see my license-plate collecting   7
phase at age eleven as a manifestation of my repressed desire to escape, to run away to a more interesting place. It is like my dreams of riding the ferry to Manhattan, and jumping off to swim to shore because it wasn't moving fast enough.

You can block out a lot of sounds with really good   8
earplugs, but not the bass guitar.

I knew about the *krampus* before it became   9
such a trendy art world thing. *Krampus* was the nickname for my Hungarian boyfriend, when he was being grouchy or stubborn. It is based on a Hungarian word for monster. And dear reader, I slept with him.

Another nickname we had for him was *shayt*   10
kukotz, cheese-worm, for when he was antsy or nervous.

Post hoc ergo propter hoc: if something happens   11
after something else, it doesn't mean the first thing caused it.

We do tend to think that because things follow   12
one another in time, they are sequential.

We had a wild moment in the heat of the town of   13
Ciénaga, after visiting the shabby monument to

the massacred banana workers. The marketplace was surrounded by peddlers, beggars, and homeless people eyeing our camera equipment. Suddenly it was 113° and our car would not start.

14   David asked me to get out and check the tailpipe in case someone had stuffed it with paper. It was so hot it was hard not to think that the town was conspiring against us, like an Orson Welles movie, like *A Touch of Evil*.

15   What about making art from boogers and fingernail clippings?

16   Basically I like the idea of "body art," using things like menstrual blood, and hair, but I think there is still further to go.

17   I remember Mary Kelly's fecal samples from her baby son. She put them on slides and featured them in her first big show.

18   David Burns had a piece with waxed strips of paper with little hairs on them from when he got his ass waxed.

19   It's not often a son can be as useful to his mother as Mary Kelly's son was.

20   Often when you return from a trip, the trip stays with you in little pieces.

21   A white elephant is a gift that seems desirable, but comes to ruin its recipient.

22   I have seen this with friends who inherited money when they were young, or had early fame, or great beauty in their youth.

23   In the 90s, my father's friend Joel went to prison for five years for growing marijuana. He had more

than a hundred plants, so they decided he was selling it even though he was a lawyer and was actually giving it away. He tried a new defense by arguing that statistically half the plants would be male, and useless. It didn't work.

Monsters will always be cool.   24

My dog Peggy didn't act very excited to see me   25
when I got home. It seems like she's pissed that I left and didn't want to seem overenthusiastic when I got back.

1

Today I woke up thinking about Jason Gould. He   1
is Barbra Streisand's son, and for a while I saw him regularly at Gold's Gym in Hollywood.

It must be hard to be Barbra's son. You couldn't   2
dream about putting your mother into a movie because she's already been in so many.

I seem to have gotten a haircut today. It was one   3
of those with a lot of combing and brushing, a snip here and there, and then the blow dryer comes out. That's why I say seem.

The hardest part for me of getting my hair cut   4
is chatting with the stylist. I never know what to say. It's the main reason I wait so long before getting my haircut.

I've seen David Burns get his hair cut, and he just   5
chirps away with the cutter. I envy that.

In Cali we met Alejandro, who is a kind of   6
shaman or witch doctor, and among other things he made a banana mandala in Nashira that no one seems to be taking care of.

7   There is a restaurant in Paris run by the blind for the benefit of the sighted. You eat in pitch darkness with the assistance of blind waiters. Why settle for another cuisine when you can eat in another world?

8   I love the idea of a restaurant in the dark, *dans le noir* as the French call it. And it is an idea, one that perhaps obliterates the possibility of experience, even as it instantiates it.

9   It reminds us how much conceptual art can be seen as grounded in allegory.

10   Nina Simone.

11   A few days ago in Colombia I had too much to list, so I stopped.

12   I saw a skunk crossing the road today.

13   The Spanish word *urgencia*, emergency, always of course makes me think of urgency, and overflow.

14   Isn't overflow the essence of our experience of reality or of being? There is too much all at once.

15   So fiction is a lie, plot lines, one thing at a time.

16   This doesn't mean experience is a mess.

17   And even the Zen thing—meditation, turning inwards, tuning in—is an artifice, a nice one though.

18   There is a carnival character in Barranquilla called Marimondo. He has two colored rings around his eyes, a ring around his mouth, and a long sausage-like nose. He looks a lot like the Jack in the Box.

Clowns are often scary. It's that mix of inanimate   19
object and monkey-like, or just animal energy.

I remember *Jonathan Livingston Seagull*. I read   20
it in junior high school and thought it was so
meaningful.

It seems to be about a seagull but it's really about   21
us, about being alive, about being.

The Amazon is the largest river system in the   22
world.

I read about it while looking up Cali, but the Cali   23
River is not in the Amazon's watershed.

Ever since I understood the continental divide,   24
watersheds seemed so important to me. The
continental divide is the place where a drop of
rain, with the tiniest variation, could end up in a
river on one side of a continent, or on the other.
It's like the idea in chaos theory that the flutter of
a butterfly wing could end up starting a hurricane
on the other side of the globe.

This seems so important, the determinant of   25
importance, or rather a system of meaning based
on difference. But it is also arbitrary, a theory.

li

Last night I read some Brecht poems aloud in   1
German at a big museum on a terrible sound
system, to the general mystification of the noisy
audience.

Unlike Spanish, German is an irrelevant language   2
in the world in which I live.

Peggy threw up this morning after I made her   3
scrambled eggs. She's scary skinny and only picks

at her vegetarian dog food. She can't have meat, so she's a prisoner of vegetarianism.

4   Sometimes I see guys I know online on gay cruising sites and I pretend I don't know them.

5   What a terrible thing, to get killed because you were out looking at Christo's *Umbrellas* and a big wind came up and knocked one of them on your head.

6   Last night I had some salmon out to grill, and when I came back in the kitchen I noticed Peggy had taken a bite out of it.

7   It's not as if she's becoming less and less of herself, but certainly a lower calorie version of herself, with less frills.

8   The most interesting thing about paint chips isn't actually the colors or their weird names, like Persian Twilight, but the numbers. How did that color become 2202E?

9   When I'm writing, I often end up with a kind of spit pile. It's pages of things I couldn't get to fit.

10   I once saw Alanis Morissette naked at Esalen.

11   Every Thursday night in the hot springs there they play the didgeridoo. They call it the "didg." You sit in the hot water naked and silent, with no light but a candle or the moon.

12   I sat naked about five feet from Alanis but I did not talk to her.

13   It's hard to write in stereo because you can't exactly push two words out at the same time, and even if you do a reader will see one and then the other.

What if Peggy dies?   14

I have a box of mangos here that might be the   15
best mangos in the world: Manila mangos, also
called Champagne or Ataulfo mangos. They're
small and yellow, and when dead ripe have a flavor
like honey, apricots, grapefruit, and champagne
grapes.

Simple allegories use simple parallelisms, complex   16
ones more profound, and the best allegories don't
appear allegorical to us at all.

I remember Earth Shoes.   17

How can you tell the difference between a   18
symptom and a personality?

This is a problem both with psychoanalysis and   19
with texts.

I often enjoy people's symptoms more than their   20
personalities.

In Colombia they have mangos and mangas, but   21
as far as we could understand the difference was
only one of size: mangas are the big ones, the ones
we mostly get from Central America.

What I like about pronouns is that in some ways   22
they have more power than proper nouns.

Pronouns are more professional. Take she, they,   23
or them, you get a pretty solid sense of where they
come from and what their job is.

Then take Peter or Pasadena versus it or him.   24

Last night I read some of his poems in German   25
there on one of those to their general mystification.

lii

1   To speak of Peggy's death is an allegory, but also not an allegory.

2   I've only done karaoke once, for a LACE benefit many years ago, but I think it is fair to say I got a boyfriend out of it.

3   Dead animals in my life include a few cats, several goldfish, two hamsters, and quite a bit of road kill.

4   None of them were as emotional as the first dead cat, which I didn't even see die. It disappeared and then one day about a month later, I came home to my brother crying because my mother told him the cat had been run over by a car.

5   The fruit I remember most from Colombia is the grenadilla. They taste cool and sweet, but the best thing about them is the seeds, which crunch in the most perfect way.

6   Death is hard and being cheated of death is just as hard, though in different ways.

7   My street has a lot of parking, few streetlights, and little traffic. Occasionally couples park there in their cars to make out or take drugs. Sometimes I hear a door slam, and yelling, but can't tell what it is about.

8   My spam email divides neatly between asking for money or offering to enlarge my penis.

9   Liz Hansen reminds me that I did a naked handstand in the showers at Esalen, of which she took a photograph.

10   When I was a kid my mother once tried to feed a squirrel in our yard. But it bit her hand and

clamped down, and I remember her beating it against a fence to get it off.

In my family we had a great love of all animals, large and small.   11

The only time I ever got flowers delivered, they   12
came anonymously, which was tremendously exciting. I decided who sent them, but then I found out they were from someone else, and everything about them seemed terribly disappointing.

For a few years we had a family of raccoons living   13
in an ancient, hollowed-out Sugar Maple tree in our backyard. We started to feed the raccoons and more and more arrived. Finally they got in a fight with our cat and mauled her. So ended that lovefest.

I remember getting a tennis ball hit into my eye   14
socket on a tennis court, and seeing stars.

It was unforgettable, though for some reason I   15
did not get a black eye.

You can tell a lot about a person by a) their   16
relationship to houseplants and b) what foods linger in their homes (and what foods disappear immediately).

There is no real magic to the number 25 the way   17
there is to the number 12 or 14, i.e. the sonnet.

Two foods that never stay long in my house are   18
ice cream and salami.

The Milky Way is my way.   19

The only thing I brought back from Colombia   20
was special coffee from a plantation atop ancient burial mounds of indigenous people.

21   While the metaphor hitches itself to the stars, the metonym's ties are mostly to itself, or something right next door.

22   The road in front of my family's house in the Catskills was called Cattail Rd. and it ran parallel with the Milky Way. It was so dark there that at night you saw all the stars, and indeed it felt a little as if we were living in the whole galaxy. The effect was compounded in the summer not only by fireflies but by little glow worms on the ground. Seen up close, the worms look like railroad cars with lit windows.

23   Email spam pierces my consciousness despite my ignoring it.

24   I know I said something about conceptual art and allegory, which is distinctly in the metaphor corner of the ring, but when I think about it, a lot of conceptual art is grounded in metonymy. You can see this easily in the chair, the picture of the chair, and the definition of the chair.

25   Of course it is easy enough to read the chair as an allegory.

liii

1   Have you noticed how fashionable randomness is right now? Random is the new black.

2   Once, in college, I caught a cute guy jerking off in the library. He was wedged on the floor in a corner and gazing at a girl he liked. She couldn't see him, but I could.

3   Metaphor and metonymy are really sloppy categories because both are about figural language.

The guy in the library really turned me on, but   4
after a minute he realized I was looking and he
jumped up and left.

If you had to make a judgment here, you would   5
say he was the pervert and not me, wouldn't you?

These lists would be more random if I took the   6
last fifty, scrambled them up, and picked twenty-
five things by chance. But even then.

I intend to let go of Peggy when the time is right. I   7
think she has a few more weeks. I'm mourning her
a little now, while she's still here to comfort me. She
seems not to be suffering, just sort of evaporating.

I'm still thinking about pronouns. Some of that   8
and those were his, while others were theirs.

When I was growing up in New York, kids would   9
use y'all, youse, you guys.

Sexual hookups on the internet have the effect of   10
seeming random, but who are we kidding?

Actually, I got flowers delivered at least twice in   11
my life, blue irises once and white lilies another
time. I remember misjudging the anonymous
sender of the irises, but now I can't remember at
all who sent the lilies.

My mother had several pepper mills and the largest   12
one was called the Rubirosa, after Porfirio Rubirosa,
a famous Latin playboy who dated Rita Hayworth
in the 50s and apparently was very well endowed.

In junior high school I knew a girl who cut   13
herself. I noticed a cut on her arm by accident
once, and she caught me looking. After that, for
a few months we had a little game in which she'd
reveal a little more to me every time she thought
I might be looking.

14   Once in our house in the Catskills my mother and father had an argument and the next morning my mother picked up a blanket and walked off into the woods. After a few hours, I found her seated on a ridge and she told me she was not coming back. I got my father to apologize to her and try to convince her to come back. It was getting dark. She told me she just intended to stay in the woods, she didn't know how long, but she didn't want to live in a house anymore.

15   I begged her at least to come sleep in the garage. There were wolves, bears, and mountain lions in the woods.

16   I'm fascinated with wasp galls. Tiny wasps lay eggs on California oak trees and the larvae build these bulbous woody nests, which look like a strange fruit.

17   They also look like testicles, smooth, beige, and flesh-like.

18   As it got dark I brought my mother some food and more blankets. I told her the garage was open.

19   Around midnight she moved into the garage, and the next day she was back in the house.

20   In junior high school I had a sort of faggy classmate named Glen Kovac who disappeared one year. We were told he'd accidentally suffocated himself on the cord of a Venetian blind. Later, kids started using the phrase "autoerotic asphyxiation."

21   I love that wasp galls are a kind of inter-species architecture: bugs building with trees.

22   The word testicle comes from the Latin *testis*, witness, as if they testify to a man's virility or something. In Roman law one witness was useless

unless his testimony was corroborated by a second witness, so witnesses in trials always came in pairs.

Isn't it weird when your legs fall asleep? 23

I remember before I learned to use "asleep" in 24
this way I would say my legs felt *kribblig* (tingly),
but also like the English word crib, as if they are
crawling back to the crib.

I'm eating these amazing kumquats that Fran 25
Bennett left in the office at CalArts. I dropped
some in the grass and they look like orange Easter
eggs.

liv

When you list things every day you create both 1
a ritual and a vacuum. Every day you fill the
vacuum, and every next day it's back.

Sometimes you look back at an ex lover and you 2
see that all the sweet qualities you once saw were
really only the qualities you chose to see.

The list becomes a kind of new orifice. First it 3
feels enormous, like a new planet or a whole new
wing on your house. Then it feels very small, like
trying to squeeze a sofa through a cat door.

When Jack Wrangler described his move from 4
starring in gay porn to straight porn, he said it
was a career move. "Why be a nurse," he said,
"when you can be a doctor?"

Anything can fit through a cat door if you chop it 5
into small enough pieces.

Imagine if we could not walk on two feet. How 6
would we multitask? Imagine not being able to
walk and talk on the phone, for instance.

7   Some people don't walk on two feet. Some people walk on all fours, though we usually don't see it. Some don't actually walk at all.

8   I was googling Brian Butler's name, because it came up in a conversation, and it seems he wrote a book called *Europe For Free!*

9   The first time I had sex was in the library at Lincoln Center. My mother and I went there together after visiting an old family friend, and then we split up because she wanted to go somewhere else.

10   I remember I was pulling books off a shelf and through the gap to the other side, I saw a man's testicles. Then I followed him to the bathroom and we sort of had sex there.

11   I knew exactly what I was doing.

12   My mother and I had visited Fritz Cassirer, a crotchety old man who was from an old Jewish Berlin family of art dealers and philosophers. I remember he had a big wooden table from the 15th century.

13   I've noticed how many tropical fruits have thick, inedible skins, like the pineapple, the mango, or the banana. The fruits of temperate climates are almost all thin and edible, like plums, cherries, or apples.

14   Fritz was my aunt's boyfriend, though he was almost thirty years older than she. He would summon us to visit, not exactly to be interrogated or to entertain him, but something of both.

15   Doubtlessly I spent a lot of time worrying about things I shouldn't have, but I'll write that book another time.

Occasionally my body seems very slovenly to 16
me, especially in meetings, where I catch myself
slouching, legs awry, leaning in all directions.

Twice this week I saw a skunk crossing the street 17
at night in my neighborhood, as I was coming
home from CalArts.

Usually I see a person's tendency to flop around 18
and stretch out on furniture as a sign of comfort
in their bodies.

The prospect of writing fifty more of these lists 19
yawns before me like a chasm.

Sometimes when you drive on the freeway in 20
California, you come through a patch of skunk
smell, especially at night. You don't know if they
are dead or if they just sprayed, but the smell, at a
distance, is intoxicating. Suddenly you know why
they put small amounts of it in perfume.

There is a stiffness about art openings. They're 21
anodyne. It's not about the art, or even the
people, just the ritual.

Last night I saw a coyote running down the street 22
near my house.

I forget so many people's names now. I'm 23
embarrassed. I'm too old. Too many faces have
sailed past me over time. Everyone turns into
water, or gas.

But wait, there's more! 24

It is true that I find some people so attractive that 25
I just run away.

lv

1   I bought leeches the other day. They came two in a bottle, black and scary-looking.

2   Once about fifteen years ago, Douglas Crimp introduced me to Eve Kosofsky Sedgwick on the street near the Strand bookstore.

3   Eve was so articulate and verbal it made me shy.

4   I remember going to Studio 54 when I was a college freshman. It soon came to look gross to me, when everything I knew was swept away by punk.

5   Sometimes I am surprised by the quantity of shit and piss coming from my body, which seems to have no particular bearing on how much I eat or drink.

6   If you watch guys at the gym, you notice a certain line of development. They start out skinny or chubby and get lean. Then they look toned, and soon enough, muscular. From there it's not usually a long time until they are heavy again, only with the weight distributed in ways that make them feel bigger in the right way.

7   Once I would come home from any trip with suitcases weighed down with books. I would pick up a book and remember where I got it, where I was. Now they all come in the mail, ordered online.

8   I am mystified by the big gym guy, always putting on weight so he seems bigger. It's so American— size as a virtue, your armor to protect you from the threatening gaze. Protect and attract.

9   My first bookstore was a few blocks from my house as a kid, and it was called The Book Nook.

I remember going to sex clubs with my friend 10
Adriano, and I don't think I ever liked them as
much before or since. Adriano and I would go off,
have sex, then sit on a sofa somewhere and cuddle
while we talked about what we did, wanted to do,
or didn't do.

Sometimes I dislike adjectives. 11

In Australia there are leeches that jump onto you 12
from bushes and trees. I wouldn't have believed it
if it hadn't happened to me twice.

There is a lot of power in monosyllabic words 13
like: hot, cold, fast, young, slick.

Or sex. 14

As you get older you start to see how faces and 15
bodies age, how a certain type of kid becomes an
adult and then a certain old person. You can look
at kids and see old people, and in old people you
can see kids.

David Burns and I bought Austin Young three 16
little chicks for his birthday.

When you're a kid you can't imagine kids as 17
anything but kids, etc.

I remember watching TV in black and white, and 18
how everyone looked somehow unfamiliar. Now
I see people I know, knew, or will know.

Like a lot of smart kids, I read a lot but I think my 19
peak period of reading was probably from eleven
to fifteen. Some weekends I didn't get out of bed.

There is nothing that expresses the force of life 20
like a little chick, hot and vibrating with energy
in your hand. You can see how they got associated
with Easter and spring.

143

21   I remember as a kid wanting to have sex with Charlton Heston in *Planet of the Apes*. Partly it was because he was near-naked for most of the movie, but the ape-animal-human thing must have had something to do with it.

22   I've spent the last few days choked on words. It's the opposite of that documentary on Kenny Goldsmith, *Sucking on Words*.

23   There is nothing random about a blank computer screen.

24   I must have read a lot in college because I remember *The Republic* and Aristotle's *Poetics* and all of what they called Western Civilization, but I don't actively remember reading.

25   Then I do remember reading all the time, right after college and when I first went to graduate school. I remember the acute feeling of not knowing enough, of having missed my chance at being educated.

lvi

1   Sometimes at home I hear train whistles in the distance. They seem to carry further at night, as if the sun creates some kind of interference for them.

2   The leeches came from a store in Echo Park and they seemed like they were alive, but by the time I finally got the courage to pull them out of the jar, they didn't move. I laid one on my arm in hopes of reviving it, but nothing happened.

3   There must be someone who hears train whistles at night and doesn't think of them as a mournful sound.

I've been killing rats outside my house for years   4
now.

An art project I wanted to do but never did involved   5
two wooden chairs, one labeled "remember" and
the other "forget," in different fonts.

When I first started killing rats, I laid poison all   6
around the yard. One day, though, I noticed a
dying rat zigzagging around the patio outside the
glass doors to the dining room where I often sit to
work. The rat skidded into the glass door with a
thump, in case I didn't notice the first time.

Even a piece of paper holds more promise than   7
a blank screen, maybe because you can roll up a
pencil inside it.

There's something sad about clever pet names,   8
like Gadget, Gizmo, Velcro, etc.

I decided it wasn't humane to poison rats, so   9
I began setting traps for them. They've been
around forever, made of steel and wood with
VIKTOR written on them in big red letters.
These dead rats are different. Their eyes are wide
open and clear, as if for one instant they have seen
something remarkable. I can't help but say it: they
look ecstatic.

All apparent openness in a text is secretly closure.   10

I have always wanted a pair of something like cats,   11
so I could name them *Echt* and *Ersatz*, German
for real and fake.

Why are all my random things in complete   12
sentences?

Clever names for coffee houses can be annoying   13
too, like Café Olé or Sufficient Grounds.

14 I am most receptive to randomness when I am least capable of registering it.

15 *Yom HaShoah*, Holocaust Remembrance Day, was on my birthday this year. I heard it on the radio, which also broadcast all the sirens in Israel sounding at ten in the morning. They sounded like ram's horns, ancient and mournful.

16 My life has become a machine for harvesting random things.

17 *Nel mezzo del cammin di nostra vita.*

18 Last week I had dinner with Caroline Bergvall and Molly McPhee, and from it I concluded that you can either say something startlingly new or very carefully repeat something old.

19 I almost never buy souvenirs when I travel. But I always take home a few rocks or pebbles, or shells sometimes. They're all different. They end up on a shelf, and over time I forget where they came from.

20 I love Caroline Bergvall's *Via*, in which she lists 48 (different) English translations of the first stanza of Dante's *Inferno*.

21 I've had a beard for almost two years, and I like it.

22 All that will be left of me when I am gone is a pile of rocks.

23 You can't get any younger, but you can get hairier.

24 Today someone I know told me that something I had warned him of long ago (a warning he ignored) was true. He told me I could say I told you so but I didn't. But I will confess that hearing it filled me with a certain amount of glee.

When I was younger, I said you can't get younger   25
but you can get blonder. But that was when I
dyed my hair.

lvii

Why are public radio shows so boring?   1

When I was little, my aunt from New Zealand   2
sent my brother a stuffed kiwi bird, which we
played with for many years.

Why do radio hosts like Ira Glass and Garrison   3
Keillor turn so quickly into parodies of
themselves?

The first inkling of perversity I remember was   4
on a city bus going to school. A guy stood above
me with an erection, and he kept poking it in his
pants. I pretended to ignore it by looking down
at my feet.

I was so excited that after I got to school, I left   5
class and ran in circles around the field to calm
down.

Prairie Home Companion is a fantasy of a simpler,   6
humbler time that always ends up saccharine or
pompous. *This American Life* takes the weird and
makes it familiar, but both shows settle down into
the banal.

You could say similar things about Sarah Vowell   7
or Sandra Tsing Loh.

I don't remember being bored as a kid, until I   8
became a teenager. Then I remember it intensely.
I remember just not knowing what to do with
myself. And the last part was new, the idea that I
could do something with myself.

9   To have a self.

10   Why is so much journalism today about journalists interviewing journalists? They seem to have given up on talking to people who actually saw or did something. Maybe journalists make better interviewees. They speak clearly and say the kind of things journalists want to hear, and unlike people with a relation to an event, they appear to have an objective opinion.

11   Christine Wertheim's cat beheads rats and lays them on her doorstep as welcome mats.

12   There is a great difference between teaching from a new copy of a book I know and an old one with my markings. All I need to see is a few of my underlines and comments and I dive immediately under the surface of the book into my reading of it.

13   Just touching my old copy brings me back to the book, as if it contained not just the text but its spirit as well.

14   Until humans and their introduced animals arrived, New Zealand was an island almost entirely devoid of mammals.

15   When my computer is not plugged into the internet, it seems like a work room and when it is plugged in, it seems like a play room.

16   What distinguishes mammals from all other animals are mammary glands, breasts, with which they feed their young.

17   When I was a kid, I volunteered at the Democratic Convention the summer Jimmy Carter was nominated.

I remember this older guy, like in his late twenties, was showing me around the Hilton Hotel. He said I looked like David Cassidy, which told me he was 1) out of touch, 2) not even looking at me, since I didn't look like David Cassidy, and 3) probably a pervert.

18

When I drive to CalArts, I pass a warehouse called Gadget Universe in Sylmar. Every time it starts me thinking.

19

The human body has a set of immutable relations between the number one and the number two. One nose, two eyes, for example.

20

What is a gadget? What isn't?

21

Imagine if a person had two penises, or one breast. See what I mean? Less is not more and more is not better either.

22

Can gadgets fill the whole universe?

23

Maybe they do. Maybe everything is a gadget.

24

Language is certainly a gadget. So is narrative, and so are lists.

25

lviii

I hear Peggy on the other side of the house, her nails clicking on the wood floor.

1

Peggy falls off the sofa every now and then, but it doesn't upset her. She climbs right back up.

2

When I graduated high school, I invited my favorite teachers to a party at my house and they all came.

3

I heard Raymond Carver read once at Beyond Baroque. He read one of his best stories, "Elephant,"

4

which is about a sucker who lends everyone in his family money and never gets it back. It ends with him speeding away in his friend's big, unpaid-for car.

5   It was really something to me, to see my teachers did think of me as a person.

6   I remember when everyone tried to write like Raymond Carver. When I first started trying to be a writer, that's all anyone told us to do.

7   I've always envied writers who can't stop writing, whose every impulse is transformed into narrative and words.

8   The other day I overheard two people discussing good jobs, bad jobs, plum jobs, and crappy jobs. I wonder how the plum has come to be the opposite of shit.

9   Have you noticed my lists are getting wordier? In the beginning they averaged 500 words or less, and now they come in at over 700.

10   I kill more words than I let live.

11   Evil rats on no star live.

12   I love palindromes.

13   But then who doesn't love palindromes?

14   The best palindrome is the word eye.

15   I read somewhere that Anne Sexton wanted "evil rats on no star live" on her tombstone.

16   I had a boyfriend in my junior year of high school. No one talked about it, but now when I look back, I think all the teachers knew and we were protected by a veil of silence.

All those poets who killed themselves!	17

I've said it before, but I love those words like   18
blood, root, honk, and rot.

Am I experimental enough?   19

I have often seen Rupert Everett at the gym. He   20
went to Gold's in LA and twice I saw him at the
Covent Garden gym in London. Not to sound
cocky, but I am sure he cruised me here or there.

Why are these lists so trying?   21

Because they demand so much and yet offer so   22
little.

In two days I'm going on my first balloon ride.   23

Every day I try to say something new, yet still   24
random. And every day I have less to say. I tire of
facts. I long for fiction.

"Self interrogation" is trying.   25

lix

When I first learned what conception was, I tried   1
to calculate the time of year I was conceived.
Since I was born in April, it was probably in
July. I remember thinking I was conceived in the
summer, in the heat of passion.

Some bird is singing outside. It must be some   2
kind of night bird.

But then I remembered that July is winter in   3
the Southern Hemisphere, which means I was
conceived in cold, damp weather.

4   One of my favorite short poems is by the surrealist Paul Eluard: *Pourquoi suis-je si belle? / Parce que mon maître me lave.*

5   Why am I so beautiful? / Because my master is washing me.

6   Overheard at CalArts, an older male professor saying to a young Asian girl: Everyone is lying to you, no one tells you the truth.

7   I'm working on a long piece for a journal called *Ex-nihilo*, out of nothing. It's a compilation of all my pathetic emails to my father, in bad German. They are all about his wife's health, his worries, his financial issues, etc., and almost every one begins with me apologizing. I'm calling it "Guilty German."

8   In all of the Americas, there is no place for watching birds like Panama. This is because every bird that moves north or south must come through there, like the neck of an hourglass.

9   I spent three days in a bird hotel in Panama, and I do not know what was more interesting, the birds or the birders.

10   There's no right way to edit "Guilty German." It's all wrong.

11   The bird hotel in Panama is in a tall round building that was once a radar post for the US military, now converted from watching airplanes to watching birds. It is built so you have a post on every level of the rainforest, from frog and sloth to monkey and Harpy Eagle, the largest and most powerful raptor in the Americas.

12   There are all these words to describe people on the move: immigrant, émigré and exile. The last two are sexier than the first one.

Exile always sounds presumptuous to me, haughty.   13

The ih and the eh are emphatic. Both signify motion toward or away, all depending on your perspective.   14

My mother collected wooden duck decoys, especially ratty old ones.   15

The earliest memory I have is of hanging upside down from a ranch fence in Argentina. It's associated with a certain musical phrase, sad, like an Albeniz guitar piece, a minor key. And a musty smell, sort of dry mildew, maybe from the wood fence. It was a sandy place and I was upside down, and looking at horses, or ponies.   16

For years this memory was very poignant to me, until once I tried to express it to someone and it lost all its magic.   17

Now it's like a memory of a memory. It looks like an upside down photo of me on a donkey.   18

Once in the 1980s, I read in San Francisco at Intersections with Roberto Bedoya, and I remember this short woman in a motorcycle jacket and blond buzz cut coming late, making noise and being embarrassed about it, and somehow I knew that it was Kathy Acker.   19

The next morning, Kathy left a message on Kevin and Dodie's answering machine, where I was staying, telling me she loved the reading. I remember feeling too shy to tell anyone, but I left it on Kevin and Dodie's machine so at least they would hear it.   20

My parents hated flags or anything that looked nationalistic. My father calls flags *bunte Lappen*, colorful rags.   21

22   I met Kathy twice after this. Once Dennis Cooper threw a party for her when she came to LA and I found her in a corner, like me, looking at Dennis's books. I remember looking at her and realizing she was interested in the books, but also that she was shy, and would have been happy if someone talked to her. So I did.

23   For a while I had a telephone in the shape of a decoy duck.

24   I remember being disappointed that I was conceived in the winter, but now I think it's fine.

25   The next time I met Kathy Acker was when I was in San Francisco at the same time as Mel Freilicher and he asked if I wanted to come to dinner. Afterwards we went over to her house, and all we talked about were books. She gave me an armful of books she'd read recently and thought I would like.

lx

1   Once I stayed overnight at my boss's house, and when I went to the bathroom, I found the toilet unflushed.

2   I didn't say anything, but I flushed before I used the toilet and again afterward.

3   Yesterday I flew in a hot air balloon with Susan Silton and fourteen other people. The best part is lying sideways in the basket as the balloon inflates and you slowly lift upright, as if the hand of God is picking you up.

4   We flew over Del Mar, California. It's very clean, with almost no people. Big houses, palm trees, swimming pools, and eucalyptus trees.

5   Some plants look better from above than below.

As a kid, I remember being fascinated with Learned   6
Hand, an American judge who is the lower court
judge most quoted by the Supreme Court.

These are the great Protestant names, like Cotton   7
Mather, the son of Increase Mather, the president
of Harvard in the 17th century. Cotton Mather
was a Puritan minister who wrote in support of
the judges of the Salem witch trials.

The only thing keeping you aloft in a balloon is   8
hot air, nylon, and a few steel cables.

It's better if you stop thinking and just look out.   9

Sometimes I go into the men's room to find a   10
toilet filled with wads and wads of toilet paper,
and in some way this fills me with more repulsion
than finding it full of shit, which, no doubt, is
beneath all that paper.

I see the horror of someone so disgusted by what   11
his body produces he buries it in an avalanche of
white paper, yet seems to forget to flush it.

The scariest time in a balloon is when you climb   12
higher than any building you know. Then you
realize you're flying in the sky held up only by a
few cords.

Sometimes I get the words dryad and dyad   13
confused. Dryads are tree nymphs and dyads are
a pair of something, but maybe dryads come in
dyads too.

To see the shit of your boss is unspeakable.   14

An apotropaic gesture is a set of words or rituals   15
for warding off evil. Knocking on wood, or saying
"you're not going to kill me" to a mugger.

16   Once I went to the Rose Bowl flea market with
      Millie Wilson and we met Barbara Kruger there.
      She made sure we understood that she was just
      there from a sort of anthropological perspective,
      not to shop.

17   We were there to shop.

18   The tetragrammaton is the unspeakable Hebrew
      name of God, transliterated into four letters as
      YHWH, and pronounced as Yahweh.

19   It is blasphemous to speak the name of God.

20   One day when I was a teenager, my father
      disappeared. He had gone to meet a friend of a
      friend at the airport and never came home. Over
      the next days, we found out that it was a woman,
      a lawyer, and they had met before in Europe, and
      he was staying in her hotel room in the city.

21   I remember my mother, brother, and I very
      rationally planning what we should do, which at
      that point involved driving to Washington, DC
      to get a divorce. I can't remember where that idea
      came from, but I think it was from my head,
      not my mother's. Washington was the place for
      official business.

22   After a week or so, when my father finally came
      home late one night, he was hungry, so I made
      him eggs and sausage. I remember throwing the
      plate down and saying, "There's your eggs!"

23   It's not windy on a balloon ride, because you are
      being pushed along with the wind.

24   Later my parents got a king size bed instead of
      their two twin beds. In my mind the big bed is
      American while the small ones are European.

Actually, they just pushed the two twin beds   25
together.

lxi

Years ago, I drove down to Derrida's classes at UC   1
Irvine. He always wore white shoes, which made
him seem kind of like a dandy.

Apparently UCI flew him around in a helicopter,   2
looking like something between an urgent care
nurse and an important doctor.

There's too much life, or too much work in my   3
life.

There's no space for the random, which requires a   4
bit of leisure to observe.

At that point Derrida was moving from his   5
lectures on cannibalism and eating the other, to
those on the friend and the enemy. One category
plays off the other, and often they merge, or
switch places.

A hot air balloon is so fat, bloated, but also thin,   6
just a membrane.

And the world is so fat! It's really big, really really.   7

One of my earliest memories is of the beach. The   8
tide was coming in, so we gathered our toys and
left. When I got home, I realized we forgot my
Barrel of Monkeys, a styrofoam barrel with plastic
monkeys you connect in a chain.

We went back to the beach the next day, and there   9
were my monkeys in a different place, washed
away by the tide but then washed up again. What
the Lord taketh away he sometimes giveth back.

10   My father assures me we did not arrive in America on a propeller plane. He says it was a jet, a De Havilland Comet 4. He sent me a picture of it.

11   I reject this. It does not fit my narrative desire.

12   I was a Derridean pretty much before I was anything else, but eventually I became disenchanted with him.

13   Or more precisely I couldn't stand the Derrideans. It was like the difference between Christ and the Christians.

14   I have many memories, from different parts of my childhood and later, of being in airplanes. It seemed like a big thing.

15   When I was a kid and went to the beach, I thought sand bars were a kind of miracle. Out there, land past the water, sort of, and sometimes you had to pass through water over your head, and then you're standing again. The passage through water to land.

16   Actually I have more memories of airports, some of them very wrenching.

17   There's something about the machinery and the people coming and going, a site of anguish, rupture, and reunion.

18   I always get sentimental at the end of the school year.

19   Today we had graduation reviews. All the MFAs work is so much better than it was when they started. Is it something the teachers did?

20   My brother and I got sent to a Lutheran church to decide if we believed in God, but after two or three years, I guess we decided we didn't. Now

I'm glad it happened because otherwise I really wouldn't understand Christians.

I kind of like the random thing.   21

Maybe anybody's writing would get better after   22
two years of working on it.

The MFA thing is a sort of self-fulfilling prophecy.   23
Poof, you're a writer.

Probably a lot of people today don't remember   24
mimeographs, those ditto sheets they'd hand
out in school, faint purple ink and smelling
like acetone. They called mimeograph machines
"spirit duplicators."

Christine Wertheim and I decided that maybe we   25
at CalArts are at least doing more than nothing.
We're definitely not doing everything, but maybe
we're doing something.

lxii

When my leg falls asleep and I can't quite walk on   1
it, it feels like my body is something other to me.

I'm not made for durational projects.   2

I'm weak.   3

When my leg falls asleep, I think of my mother's   4
left leg, which was amputated six years before she
died.

Allen Ginsberg wrote *Kaddish* for his mother's   5
death.

The actual Kaddish was never spoken by mourners   6
but only by the rabbi.

7   Another meeting with a curator.

8   I can't tell you more.

9   I looked it up, and I was surprised to find the traditional Kaddish is more about God's name and never mentions the dead nor even death.

10   That's not the kind of Kaddish I would write for my mother either.

11   My name means "gift of God." My parents picked it because it worked in both Spanish and German (and Portuguese, and Finnish), but it doesn't much exist in English.

12   In German it is usually spelled Matthias, which is the adaptation of the Greek name Matthaios (same as Matthew), which was an adaptation of the Hebrew Mattiyahu, gift of Yahweh, or God.

13   The Germans are big into modernizing archaic spellings of things. At least they were, once.

14   I remember one of the most horrible academics I studied with was Ann Bergren, who taught a class on the pre-Socratic roots of Post-Structuralist thought. After a semester of reading mostly Derrida, I realized that what she wanted was not a paper written the way Derrida would write, but an academic paper that put Derrida's ideas into a scholarly argument. She wanted me to prove something.

15   This was a big crisis for me.

16   Plop, plop, fizz, fizz. Oh what a relief it is.

17   LACMA, MOCA, LACE, MOMA, MALBA, MAMBO. All these museums or art spaces known by their acronyms. It's like baby talk.

But it's very serious baby talk, or pidgin: a 18
simplified language developed between two
groups who don't understand each other.

I was driving home last night and on the radio 19
I heard the father of a two-year-old boy who
died eighteen years ago by drowning. The family
brought his body home in a wooden chest and
kept him there to mourn for three days before
his funeral.

It was the day after CalArts graduation reviews 20
and I was still thinking about the amount of pain
in the students' work. Everywhere, the cruelty of
families, of children, of lovers.

I pulled the car over and started sobbing. 21

Pidgin is the Chinese alteration of the English 22
word "business."

Eventually we all live through terrible things, or 23
we die from them.

Flowers are restful to look at. They have neither 24
emotions nor conflicts. —Sigmund Freud

For the most part, the flowers I like are the 25
irregular ones, not the daisies or the carnations. I
like orchids, for example, pansies, and calla lilies,
the furthest from a lump shaped rose or anything
shaped like a dinner roll.

lxiii

The flowers I like look like p's and q's, or k's, 1
instead of the normal ones like o's or asterisks.

I have an ongoing struggle with Kathy Acker's 2
Wikipedia page. Readers come along with some
regularity to edit her biography, and the one thing

they often insert is that she worked as a prostitute in her twenties.

3   I like flowers that look like tears or hats or babies in a cradle, that suckle to their stems like piglets. I like the flowers that look like question marks, the ones that flap in the wind almost like mistakes.

4   My mother's ashes stayed in their cheap container for two years after her death. We knew we wanted to scatter them in the woods by the house, but my father, brother, and I were never there together.

5   Finally just before my father moved away to remarry, he and my brother impetuously scattered the ashes and then called to tell me. I was unspeakably angry about it.

6   Now and then I go to Wikipedia and remove the mentions of Kathy working as a prostitute. She didn't. She worked as an erotic dancer or a stripper, and then for only a year or so.

7   I sat with my anger for a few weeks and didn't speak to either my brother or my father.

8   But finally I forgave them. Ashes are nothing, and that's their point. Nothing is left of us when we are gone.

9   One of my teaching fantasies is that my students become so absorbed in their discussion they don't need me. After I ask a few questions, they start talking so intensely that I can sink under the table. For the rest of the class I sit under the table and just listen to them be brilliant.

10 Kathy's experience as a stripper and the stories she heard from the women she worked with, stories of sex abuse, rape, and prostitution, were formative to her understanding of gender in America.

My mother made me cry as a child when she said that she wanted to be cremated when she died and would be happy if a little plant grew from her ashes. 11

Don't worry, I'll make time. 12

There's something about the role of artists at CalArts… nowhere else would you gather to listen to artists expound on politics, like after 9/11. 13

Imagine gathering at the feet of political scientists to hear about art. 14

I know guys who call their penises their peter, or their little winkie. Maybe it's not that bad, until you realize they don't quite mean it as a joke. 15

And then there are words like boo-boo or ouchie. If I had a cut I would probably just say cut, or burn, or bruise. But of course I love those words too, the way boo-boo kind of naturally leads to bon-bon. 16

For a minute, I saw myself as an animal looking in the window from outside would see me—as a species dedicated to activities that have no measurable relationship to its survival. 17

Today is the ten-year anniversary of my mother's death. 18

About the only thing I can say for sure is that by now it's clear that she is dead and I am alive. 19

Kathy would not have minded being called a prostitute, but I remove it from the record because the record should be factual. 20

My mother died the day after Mother's Day, which was the last day I talked to her. I was planting apple trees at a house in the Los Padres mountains. 21

22   It was on a cordless phone and I really was planting apple trees while I talked to her, phone cradled to my ear as I dug.

23   She called me, actually thinking she had dialed my brother, who called her earlier. So the last time we talked, she first called me by my brother's name, Valentin.

24   The stories the prostitutes told her echoed through Kathy's work for the rest of her life.

25   It's nice that I can still hear my mother's voice. I like that. I hear it over the telephone though, not live.

lxiv

1   What is my mother like as a dead person? Is she wiser?

2   Last week I videotaped a set of interviews for the writing position at CalArts. The writers were interesting, but I kept wishing I could turn the camera on the committee, to capture us in unknowingness.

3   My first shopping mall was the Staten Island Mall, which was then "anchored" by a Sears and Macy's—sort of sensible and fancy, by our standards.

4   The announcer on the classical radio station has a voice inside his voice; he sort of swallows his words as if his voice is not really his.

5   Something else is there.

6   My mother had the capacity to reflect, but even more she had the power of cognition and connection.

It's hard to imagine how those powers work for dead people. 7

Earlier, I was admiring the bulging upper arm of a student. The muscles are plump but his skin is speckled like a plucked chicken. 8

We were dazzled by the mall thing, and I remember thinking what an improvement it was on 34th St., which was anchored by Macy's and B. Altman's with crummy old New York stores like Korvettes, A&S, and Gimbels, where Lucy and Ethel shopped. 9

Miranda Mellis says, "The monster is the message." 10

I admired the B. Altman and the Lord & Taylor logos and tried to style my handwriting after them. 11

My mother heard voices in her head. I mean she had bad memories, not voices telling her what to do. 12

Pineapples are sweeter on the bottom than on the top. The sugar sinks. 13

On really sensitive microphones, the noise of someone moving the cable gets recorded; even the wind on the cable can be audible. 14

Cough syrup is so powerful! Either that or I am so weak. 15

I'd like to do a project in which I dangle a good microphone cable out the window with the mic muted, to see what ambient movement it would pick up. 16

Peggy turns in circles before she lies down to sleep, a kind of landing pattern. 17

18   There's a certain attentiveness I feel when I work a video camera. I see how the camera registers things. I don't just see as me, but as the camera.

19   How are writers and poets going to narrate the bailout?

20   Cristina Garcia says of her work, "You're reading it in English but hearing it in Spanish."

21   So no, death did not make my mother wiser, only quieter.

22   Henry James said that words are like irritants, what the oyster uses to make the pearl.

23   In different light, I can look either healthy or unhealthy.

24   For a time when I was in college, my mother was very interested in the question of prostitution. Once she and my father were in Times Square and they met a prostitute and took her to dinner and talked to her.

25   Kathy Acker and I once went to a pet cemetery in the desert. We loved it. She noticed how much more people loved their animals than each other.

lxv

1   I've been looking at the sex ads online and I'm struck by both the variety of people's pleasures and their monotony, the slavish repetition.

2   This is the problem of genre.

3   Walking outdoors, I will grab a leaf of whatever plant I pass and crush it to see what it smells like.

I just poked a lymph node in my neck, which is 4
swollen from my cold, and I decided that maybe
homeopathic medicine does work. You give a
tiny amount of poison to stimulate your body to
respond to the disease.

This is a realization best made while high on 5
cough syrup.

In the sex ads there is a kind of arcana or lore, as 6
encoded as medieval scholasticism.

My mother was raised by her grandmother and 7
they were poor. For several years she worked as
a housecleaner in a bordello owned by her rich
aunt.

She told me she liked the women there, and they 8
were always very kind to her.

Why is no one talking about poor people? 9

Random things are what irritate; what makes the 10
oyster makes the pearl.

The newspaper is filled with stories about 11
the Great Recession, but no one seems to be
complaining, or depressed.

This must be a very upbeat downturn. 12

In general people have a bias in favor of certainty, 13
or things we believe exist.

This is my problem with a certain amount of 14
conceptual art, its favoring of that which exists
over that which does not.

An exercise for guys. Look at your body. Imagine 15
your shoulders narrowing and your breasts
coming forward. How does it feel?

16   Democracy is a concept. I have never actually lived in a full democracy.

17   All democracies so far are partial.

18   Never since ancient Greece and Rome has there been such a robust public display of phalluses. They're everywhere online.

19   Allegory is like camp. It's either intentional (on the part of the writer or artist) or a product of reading.

20   Therefore anything can be allegorical.

21   The gloryhole: now there is a word to behold.

22   As my mother aged, she began to dislike her body. Once she came to the desert with me and my boyfriend and after we had to drag her into the Jacuzzi, she said it was "not aesthetical" for people to have to see an older person's body like this.

23   Reading sex ads online, I think that the misspellings often make them sexier, up to a point.

24   I often think of more things after I finish working on random things for the day than while I am thinking of random things for that day.

25   The phenomenon of including cock shots rather than a picture of yourself when you're looking to give a blow job has always interested me.

lxvi

1   There are certain phrases that never sound quite right, like "I want to get naked with you." Or "sexy time," "make whoopie," "have nooky." Oh, and "sex maniac." I love that term.

Today I've eaten three oranges and each one   2
tasted slightly different.

The Atlantic side of the Panama Canal is 76 feet   3
higher than the Pacific side, and I often wondered
what would happen if you built a tunnel and all
the water rushed from one ocean to another.

When I saw *Einstein on the Beach* so long ago, it   4
created a new kind of performance art for me.
Because I was being seduced by the man sitting
beside me, I wasn't just an audience. I was a
participant.

Let's leave behind the old avant-garde. The white   5
cube and the black monolith—like the one at the
beginning of *2001: A Space Odyssey*, which excites
all the apes until they learn to use tools, a bone,
which they then use to kill each other.

Also, what if we used the Pacific to fill up Death   6
Valley, which is 224 feet below sea level?

My father took me to see *2001* as a kid. I   7
remember I was fascinated but confused, and I
had nightmares later about monkeys under my
bed, waiting to pull me down.

Occasionally I have come across pictures of me   8
on gay sex sites being presented by other men as
themselves.

If you read these lists you will probably know   9
everything you will ever need to know about me.

Doesn't everyone have a monkey under their bed?   10

Recently at school I met with Orlando Tirado,   11
who is photographing all kinds of gay men's
bodies naked, in what he calls describing the
indescribable.

12   *2001* the movie and *2001* the novel were created at the same time; neither is an adaptation of the other, but they are not the same.

13   I just had a vision of the future, and it looks like my blood on a piece of paper.

14   I mean that's what led to my vision.

15   Have you ever seen light shadows? Like when you watch a dark figure on a light background, on a stage or a dais, and you look away and you see the figure in reverse everywhere you look.

16   It's as much a dark shadow I guess. It's something you see when you read against the grain.

17   I will confess I often find repressed people sexier than promiscuous ones.

18   Maybe it is the challenge of repression.

19   In my recollection, it seemed very important to my father for us to see *2001* together. Now I think of *2001* as being important to my father, as though it says something about him.

20   I have a complicated system for saving random things, which involves keeping a paper folded in quarters in my pocket all the time, then transcribing the things to my computer, then putting together the old things as I continue to write the new things.

21   After years of problems with circulation, my mother's leg was amputated. She was tough. She told me that a prosthetic leg that works is better than a real one that doesn't.

22   Yesterday I chanced upon the sex ad of a long-ago ex. He's lying even more than I am.

All the Oedipal narratives are about limping somehow, and about the limpid, and the limpet.   23

Isn't it curious how fruit can refer to both an individual thing and a category, one fruit and all fruit? And like the word gay, fruity once had a more innocent meaning.   24

It is interesting that we don't seem to think of homosexuality as innocent.   25

lxvii

Keith Hennessy says the greatest response he got on Facebook was this week when he questioned the meaning of "friend."   1

I remember the first time I went to Paris and saw a *pissoir* (a public urinal). It seemed like a civilized wonder, so I photographed it. A woman who was passing by saw me, and called me a "*sale cochon*," a dirty pig.   2

I just reread a few dozen lists and I see that so much has been omitted.   3

David Burns and I sometimes call people on Facebook "frenz."   4

I am using the most obvious devices here: mixing genres or styles, for example pairing the sentimental with the obscene.   5

Or anticipating commentary, rephrasing it, and thereby foreclosing it, which makes the work seem more rounded or rooted or sweeping somehow.   6

I remember when Friendster came around and I felt the name was right. Not friends but friendsters, a little sinister perhaps, like gangster.   7

8 Or by mixing ordinary with extraordinary, irreverence with sincerity, brutality with sensitivity, or present and past with future.

9 You know, one of my favorite words of late is chillax.

10 The worst is MySpace, which is less about friends than adolescence and narcissism.

11 There's music in that word, chillax.

12 Are there forms of friendship which are not narcissistic?

13 Can I tell you something kind of gross?

14 Often when I'm really busy working, I have a large plastic jug at my desk and I just pee in it to avoid a trip to the bathroom.

15 So many sex ads say they are actually looking for a "deeper connection."

16 My mother never mastered her prosthetic leg, but it was never far away. When she rolled around in her wheelchair she kept it on her lap.

17 Keep your friends close and your enemies closer. That's an ancient quote though lots of people think it's from *The Godfather*.

18 I'm two-thirds through now. I can see the end and am starting to feel like I have too much to fit in.

19 I'm giving up on not knowing what will come next.

20 As I sit here, I hear kids outside playing, screaming at each other. Anything could be happening.

Self-consciousness or reflectivity on process   21
is a sure winner. As are name dropping and
embarrassing revelations.

John Cage's book *Indeterminacy* is composed   22
of random stories that are connected primarily
through a certain attitude.

I remember in high school when all the girls' hair   23
had "wings."

Recently at school I met with Henry Crouch,   24
who is photographing gay cruising areas and
parks, what he calls the un-representable spaces
of desire.

Things I could touch from where I am sitting: 25
pens, iPhone, computer and cables, dried rose
petals, messy stacks of paper, and a plastic jug half
full of urine.

lxviii

In high school, I became a sort of junior Marxist,   1
read all these books, and wrote a long paper for
my economics class. My teacher said the paper
was too good for me to have written it myself.

I never thought of my piss jug as a chamberpot   2
but I like the comparison. I always liked the term
"night water."

Death to the capitalist insect that preys upon the   3
life of the people!

Peggy is getting thinner all the time and only   4
picks at her food, so every day I confect new ways
to get her to eat.

I remember a formative moment when I was   5
fourteen and I saw graffiti on a city courthouse

that said "faggots unite against patriarchy." I remember I had to look up patriarchy, but not faggot.

6   My failure in writing here lies in the structure of the 25: the catchy opening, and the apposite ending. I can resist closure but I can't resist apposition.

7   My brother and I had many stuffed animals. My first one was a bear that I got for Christmas four months before I was born.

8   Chamberpots make me think of bedknobs and broomsticks.

9   My mother loved Steiff stuffed animals. We had a family of porcupines who walked upright and wore clothes. They got put away so they wouldn't get damaged.

10   I saw a John Cage piece once at CalArts when I first started teaching there. Cage sat at a desk on the stage writing on paper, and occasionally he'd read a number out loud. He was balancing his checkbook.

11   In retrospect the stuffed porcupines were toys my mother never had as a kid, so she got them for us and then locked them away.

12   Peggy hates her dog food, which has no meat. The vet said meat protein gives her crystals in her bladder, which make her incontinent.

13   The father of the stuffed porcupine family was named Mecki, almost like Mackie Messer in *The Threepenny Opera*.

14   Kurt Weill was a big part of my childhood, all that music.

The word window comes from "wind eye," which   15
is very nice and always reminds me of wind socks.

A few years before she died, my mother was   16
sorting out the house and all the stuffed animals.
Once when my brother and I were visiting, she
pulled them out and we divided the pile, and now
I have half and my brother has half, including my
mother's animals.

When I finish this, will it forever change my way   17
of thinking, writing, or being? Or is that what
Jung calls compensation?

Reading the newspaper lately I've noticed how fond   18
we are of depressed, suicidal people with famous
parents and troubled lives, and how depressed
poor people don't seem worth paying attention to.

I have a wish-demand to forever change my way   19
of thinking, writing, and being.

There's a book on organizing that everyone   20
recommends, and I even bought it. But I can't
bear to read it, so it just sits there: *The 7 Habits of
Highly Effective People.*

There's something galling about the phrase   21
"highly effective."

Speaking of alienation, one of my favorite loan   22
words is *ostranenie*. It's Russian for making strange,
like the German *Verfremdungseffekt,* or alienation
effect.

The thing about any alienation effect is that to   23
work it requires something familiar.

One of my favorite definitions of depression is as   24
the inability to sustain useful delusions. Such as:
everything will be ok, people are basically kind,
or everything has a meaning.

25   One week Peggy likes eggs, then not. Another
       week it's dog biscuits, or avocados. Right now she
       only loves blue cheese.

lxix

1   I had my tooth pulled this morning.

2   Yesterday I saw a sex ad in which the guy wrote he
       was into poem instead of porn.

3   The hot water heater broke two days ago and sent
       buckets of hot water leaking through the ceiling
       and walls. It exploded like a warm can of soda.

4   For the last 24 hours I had an astonishing
       toothache. It's worse on the upper teeth because
       it's in your head more than your jaw. Your tooth
       becomes your head, the pain becomes your mind.

5   I remember when the space shuttle Challenger
       exploded, the exhaust trail wound up looking
       like a big intestine. Something about that event
       marked the end of an era.

6   Next door to my father and his wife live Nicholas
       and Elizabeth, who are both dowsers. They
       don't just work with divining rods to find water.
       Dowsing is for everything.

7   I looked up the SLA and discovered that yes,
       "death to the fascist insect that preys upon the life
       of the people" was their slogan. It probably got
       muddled in my junior Marxist head.

8   I forgot that Peter Gordon and Kathy Acker
       recorded their SLA tapes in the 70s. I must have
       heard them at some point, which kept that phrase
       circulating in my mind.

There's a different kind of space in your mouth.   9
Upper or lower, left or right, front or back. It's a
conceptual space.

I've talked to Nicholas and Elizabeth a few times   10
about dowsing. It's less a craft than a philosophy.

Dowsers work with intuition and clairvoyance,   11
and their principles apply to everything around
us.

All plumbing is really just the management of   12
the uncontrollable: our bodily waste but also the
power of nature, controlling floods.

Now the workers upstairs are pulling out the   13
old water heater and putting in a fancy tankless
heater that never leaks and does everything
better.

Where would you mark the end of the 20th   14
century? Many people said Victor Hugo's funeral,
in 1885, marked the end of the 19th.

I think it's the space shuttle Challenger explosion,   15
101 years after Victor Hugo's death.

Either that or John Lennon's assassination.   16

The old tooth will be replaced by a new one,   17
which does everything better.

In the dowsing world, nothing is random.   18

Even before the surgeon brought up the   19
mastectomy, he wanted to talk to Kathy about
breast implants. Kathy was offended by this.

Like so many non-rational systems, dowsing   20
seems to have emerged from medieval Germany.

21   Why do people think of Germans as being so rational?

22   After her mastectomy, all Kathy wanted were nipples tattooed on her chest.

23   She told a few women, including her psychic, that she never liked her breasts.

24   Some of them thought this was a big problem. Georgina, the psychic, told Kathy that she was attacking her femininity.

25   I think bilingualism builds better brains.

lxx

1   It's a good thing we do not judge the public life of a nation through the quality of its public toilets.

2   When Camille was about eight, we had a game that began with her saying, "I would be a dog, and you would be my master." After that she would bark and jump, and my job was to placate or tame her.

3   Today I was walking in front of someone I knew was watching me. I could feel him through the back of my head. I felt him looking at me. I saw my head from behind.

4   "I would be a dog" was mostly about Camille's rebelliousness and your resistance. Or her subjugation and your mercy as her master.

5   On Sunday I was on a panel with two people from the Echo Park Time Bank, where people "bank" time doing things for each other, to set up a barter system that works without cash. They said that their big problem was hoarders. People who do things for others but never ask for help, so they're hoarding credits.

Peggy is barking in her sleep. She does this when   6
she has dog dreams. Also she runs, sort of. Her
paws go back and forth. And she digs for things.

Camille's favorite stuffed animal arrived via envy.   7
One of our friend's kids had a plush black tiger
and she pined after it for weeks. But after she got
her tiger, it was her favorite animal for the rest of
her childhood.

When I drive, I see in a line 50 feet ahead and   8
sometimes I project myself into it like an arrow,
and then behind me too. This way I become a
line, just a mark on a plane.

Last week I took a walk around CalArts, around   9
the building itself. I began to think about the
difference between CalArts as an idea and CalArts
as an environment.

What's the difference between walking clockwise   10
and counterclockwise?

Kathy Acker loved her stuffed animals. For a long   11
time animal number one was a rat: "Ratty." Then
there was a goat, a shark, and an octopus. I still
have the goat.

The Time Bank only works if the barter system   12
stays in motion. My hour helping you weed is
worth your hour doing my taxes, but if everyone
helps and never asks for help, then the system is
half frozen.

When she was ten, Camille described her brain to   13
me. It was like a house, with a library, a cellar, and
an attic. Some rooms were dark and some were
bright. Some were too damp or cold, and no one
ever went inside them.

14   My brother and I played with stuffed animals for
      years. We'd have tea parties for them and for some
      reason our names at this time would be Lila and
      Maria. We fed them Hostess cupcakes, Sno Balls
      and HoHos.

15   There's a gesture of dropping things into the wind
      as you drive, leaving everything behind. I'm ready
      to leave things behind.

16   I remember seeing ads for Hostess Twinkies when
      I was a kid. They were cartoons, and Batman
      or Casper the Friendly Ghost would pacify his
      opponents with a Twinkie.

17   Pica is an eating disorder that involves habitually
      eating non-nutritive substances, like peeling
      paint or rubber cement.

18   I remember my brother no longer wanted to be
      Lila. He said there was something wrong with it.

19   The German word for an injection is *Impfung*.
      The power of the "mpf" seems greater than that
      of "unj."

20   An exclamation my mother would often use is
      the word *Pfui*. It's kind of like phooey (are they
      related?) but it's more like fie or yuck. It's that
      same "pf," pushing out.

21   A movie that made a big impression on me was
      Anastasia, the story of the woman who claimed
      to be the last surviving member of the Russian
      royal family.

22   I would play Anastasia with our cat, Blackie. She'd
      be the baby princess, wrapped tightly in a blanket.
      I'd be the grand duchess, trying to smuggle her
      out of Russia (my room) so the Bolsheviks would
      not kill her.

It's always nice to come home to a bowl of 23
cherries.

The only thing I remember about studying with 24
Tzvetan Todorov in college is that he told us to
beware of coherence. When you read something
that is too coherent, watch out; it's dogmatic.
Coherence signals a problem.

After the '94 earthquake, I remember thinking 25
everyone I knew was dead and that my
punishment had been to survive.

lxxi

I'm celebrating the departure of one of my 1
colleagues, the worst colleague and perhaps one
of the most dangerous people I have ever known.
A terrorist.

Peggy is so bony. I feel her at night, her skeletal 2
self. Soft hair, breathing, breaths like thoughts.

Nothing in the universe is like Peggy's ears. 3

The existential terrorist hides behind the law, for 4
which he actually has contempt.

He uses the rules against themselves, and he gets 5
the enforcers of rules to either pity him or fear him.

I got a call from a friend of my cousin Susana. He 6
told me she and her girlfriend were in a bad car
accident, are in the hospital, can't talk now, and
don't remember how they got there.

I wish I could be like a dog, just drop down and 7
have a nap any time.

Instead, my head is infested with words like fleas. 8

9   An existential terrorist plays the weakest person against the strongest. The weak one becomes a projectile aimed at the strongest.

10 He knows you have to get close to those you seek to destroy.

11 More than a few times, a publisher I once worked with canceled meetings because his cousin was in the hospital, or one of his cousins had just been shot.

12 Peggy's natural impulse seems to be to get under the covers with me. The bed is like a womb, but also a veil between being asleep and being awake.

13 The existential terrorist compensates for lack of firepower by either using knives or poison.

14 He claims to be the victim rather than the aggressor, especially when he is being most aggressive.

15 Dogs love their sleep.

16 An existential terrorist always chooses the power of destruction over the power to create.

17 Peggy's so thin she's more like a Whippet than a Dalmatian.

18 He scorns anyone's claims of victimization, and sees them as feeble ploys to gain power.

19 I stroke Peggy's hair like I'm playing an instrument.

20 I am little and Peggy's giant body is curved around me like a movie theater.

21 The existential terrorist de-legitimizes all other forms of interpretation.

He is the id masquerading as the superego.　22

I dreamt I was poor and eating ketchup from a　23
packet and liking it.

I was living with my father, who had his leg　24
amputated like my mother.

Peggy is all rib cage and spine, a jagged blob.　25
Melting away and getting pointy at the same
time.

lxxii

Does anyone remember the polysexuality issue of　1
Semiotext(e)? The German issue and the Nietzsche
issue were cool, but polysexuality really blew my
mind.

I just talked to Peggy's vet and she probably has　2
cancer.

Sylvère Lotringer was so sexy when I was in　3
college. He always wore a motorcycle jacket
and had a shaved head, like the biker on the
polysexuality cover, which Sylvère edited.

I'm not going to do any thing else with the vet,　4
like x-rays, or chemo. It doesn't matter to me
where the cancer is. I already knew it was there
somehow.

If I were a hundred years old like she is, in dog　5
years, I wouldn't do it for me either.

Unlike so many writers and artists, Victor Hugo　6
moved from conservatism to liberalism as he
aged.

Where does the terrorist go when he leaves? Into　7
limbo. Terrorists don't exist without institutions.

8   People come through the world and leave a wake behind them. Some leave a black wake.

9   There used to be a picture of me (a Polaroid?) on my refrigerator with Annie Sprinkle's breasts on my head. It was part of her performance.

10   I also looked inside her cervix with a flashlight.

11   We're going to put Peggy on steroids and an appetite stimulant, so she can gain some weight.

12   If you look at gay sites you'll discover an epidemic of "freeballing": guys walking around without underwear because it turns them on to be seen and/or see other guys' balls jiggling around.

13   The other word for it is to "go commando," from soldiers not wearing underwear to prevent chafing.

14   A few years ago, maybe ten, David Burns and I made absinthe and laudanum. All these quirky things you once think only interest you are soon enough discovered and marketed. Like plastic dinosaurs or dead insects preserved in frames. Like *Grey Gardens*.

15   All the fabulous ruined and faded things. All the cool, hip and fabulous things from other times, like Dorothy Parker or Tijuana Bibles.

16   I remember going rowing in Central Park with Tom Kalin and his very muscular, tattooed boyfriend who was in a hot short video called "Skinfuck" or something. It was a simulation of him jamming his shaved head up another guy's ass.

17   I told the doctor I'd rather Peggy had a good short time left than a long lousy time. That's what I'd want for me, too.

Once I visited Bob Flanagan in the hospital with 18
Eileen Myles. It was a year or two before he died
and he had been in the hospital so often, I thought
more about his hospital bed performances than
his having cystic fibrosis.

In the 90s I brought Carol Leigh, aka The Scarlot 19
Harlot, to CalArts. She's an artist and prostitute
rights advocate who first coined the term "sex
worker." There's a picture of her in her Scarlot
Harlot costume with the president of CalArts.
In my mind I kept thinking of the headline:
"College president seen with known prostitute."

The freeballing thing is the opposite of what it 20
seems. It's uptight and repressed.

Even though I knew it, I'm still crying. Peggy is 21
looking at me and thinks I'm upset about me and
not about her. She is probably right.

It was past my TV-loving years, but I remember 22
that Angela Lansbury TV show, *Murder She
Wrote*. The key moment each week is after they
find a body and Angela exclaims, "Murder?"

In literary criticism, the term burlesque describes 23
any imitative work that derives humor from an
incongruous contrast between style and subject.

I am so tired of the gelled hair look in young men, 24
out there between wind-tousled and electroshock,
with an excess of hair product to keep it forever
erect.

Oh, my little dog. 25

lxxiii

I've been saving hairballs from the shower. They're 1
in a row on the sink, drying out.

2   I'm sorting through old keys in my drawer. Some of them must be 30 years old and most of them don't open any locks I can find. They're in a tangle, tarnished and sticky; old keychains with paper tags no one can read anymore.

3   25: why do they call it two bits? Why not two and half?

4   Random: if you're working at it, you're not doing it right.

5   Peggy does not like to be picked up for a hug, but she doesn't mind if she thinks I need to carry her somewhere. So if I need to hug her, I carry her from one place to another in the house.

6   I hear the hand of the clock in the kitchen. Every second it says, "tsk, tsk, tsk."

7   Peggy's steroids seem to be kicking in already. Oh, the power of hormones.

8   Things: unity, atomization, discreet entities. These are often arbitrary, so it means getting the arbitrary right.

9   About: hitting the target.

10   Two names that seemed uncomfortably close to each other are Habitats for Humanity and Habitrails, housing for poor people and housing for hamsters.

11   I can only remember buying one stuffed animal in my adult life, because it so intrigued me. At IKEA they had a stuffed chicken with a stuffed egg you could stick back inside and pull out.

12   Can you get any more Fort-Da than that?

Me: a cloud.   13

Too: two, doubling, the first step in repetition.   14

Lately, I have more hair sprouting from my ears.   15
They're like whiskers.

Should I throw away the dead keys?   16

100 is about closure, the decimal system, and the   17
dollar bill. 100 is about America.

Do you keep the keys of the dead or do you throw   18
them away?

Right now Peggy is interested in dairy again, so   19
I have crema Mexicana, crema Salvadoreña, and
sour cream for her. I can explain the difference if
you like.

From Pic n' Save to picnic—it isn't very far.   20

I remember a scene, I think it's from *A Tree Grows   21
in Brooklyn*, with a mama's boy who is still nursing
on his beleaguered mother. When she can't take it
anymore, she puts black shoe wax on her breast
and paints a face on it.

She pulls it out, the boy runs away screaming,   22
and suddenly he is completely weened.

I think of this somehow in conjunction with   23
student-teacher relationships.

Do I remember this or am I making it up in my   24
crack-addled mind?

A hodgepodge versus a potlatch.   25

lxxiv

1   For a long time, I had a Swatch with quite a loud tick. Sometimes I'd be sitting on the toilet and hear this ticking only to realize it was me.

2   The Swatch seemed to be saying, "tsk, tsk, tsk," kind of like it pitied me.

3   I'm sorry I haven't written you sooner. I've been sick. I've been traveling. I've been buried with work. I lost your address.

4   My hands are two things: my hand writing and my fingers typing.

5   I'm right-handed, but when I type my left hand is dominant: the ASDER vs. the UGH or PHOO of handwriting.

6   We are all laterally warped.

7   Oh the capacity of my own mind to entertain me, to bore me, to soothe me, to worry me.

8   In this list of random things I'm aiming for a kind of administrative aesthetics. I want the systematic unfolding you see in conceptual art sometimes, and not an unfolding based on expression, or subjectivity.

9   No emotion, no identity.

10   Years ago, I discovered how good it is to pick berries.

11   The first time I was a child. The second time was as an adult, after college. I was in the country with my friend Nancy, who had just come home from a year in France, where she had been raped. We were picking red currents and it got late, so

we used a flashlight. They looked like rubies. We lost our balance, fell into the bushes, and couldn't get up, we were laughing so hard.

It's therapeutic, just you and the berries. It's a task with a purpose. 12

Sometimes from my house I can see fireworks at Dodger Stadium. 13

They ought to create a sort of therapy farm, where you come to pick berries, make jam, rake leaves, etc. 14

Sometimes I can see why people want to be robots, or listen to electronica, or take crystal meth. Just to be a machine, ticking. 15

Today Peggy had Fettuccine Alfredo with whole wheat pasta. She prefers human food to dog food. So do I. 16

I remember Kathy Acker peeing in the sun in the Central Valley on our way to Tijuana. I got a van with a nurse to drive from the Bay Area to Mexico. Halfway down the 5 Freeway, Kathy needed to pee, so we lowered her out to squat in a gravel parking lot. 17

When Kathy was peeing, she said, "Oh the sun feels so good on my pussy!" 18

We were on our way to an alternative cancer clinic where she died after six weeks. 19

The things people say: I've always been monogamous until now. 20

I was drunk. I never come here. I never do this. 21

22   Nikki Halpern sent me this review of Jeffrey Masson's new book on vegetarianism, *The Face on Your Plate*.

23   It starts with the reviewer's testimony as to how and when she went vegetarian, stating, "I now read books like Masson's to deepen and sustain my commitment."

24   My mother always said Americans don't like any meat that has a face on it.

25   She didn't especially like seafood, but she did like a whole fish smiling up at you from its plate.

lxxv

1   John Cage says that buzz you hear when you go into a silent room is your nervous system.

2   Sometimes mine is singing.

3   I think the nervous system is arranged in a spiral around us, like the galaxy.

4   Or like Peggy asleep around her nose.

5   Sometimes I wake up at night in the buzz of a divine insight or hunger. Literal hunger, I mean— so easy to confuse with spirituality.

6   I can imagine starving myself sometime, just to see what happens. Craving food, water, salt, waking up buzzing, stark raving mad.

7   Sometimes the only thing guiding you is the intoxication of your own mind.

8   I twitch my toes back and forth to remind myself that I am here. The span from my head to my toes is a bridge. That's the word I use, but that word is only language.

The bridge between mania and depression spans the universe, if you just pay attention. 9

Sometimes it is too much to ask of us to pay attention. 10

It's too expensive. 11

Oh, I am having the best little apricots. Velvety, and perfumed. From one side some of them look like bare butt cheeks. 12

The buzz in your head may be a virus—not a language from outer space. 13

My head, your head, his head, her head, our head, their head. 14

There are very few questions to which the answer is not: maybe you should have something to eat. 15

Sometimes you don't know if you are losing your cold or if it is getting worse. 16

David Burns doesn't love himself the way I love him. 17

All you need is a pen and paper on your bed, a dog, a phone, and a roll of toilet paper. 18

Both Peggy and I are old. Older inside than we look. But we're being reborn every minute, like the starchild in *2001: A Space Odyssey*. 19

My bed is a little star. 20

I remember Eileen Myles, when she was staying at my house a few years ago, turning to tell me how we were in our fabulous middle age. And I remember thinking, "We?" 21

22   Growing up in the East with all that underripe fruit has given me a love for tart, firm peaches and apricots. I'm still working on liking mangoes the way my Brazilian and Indian friends like them, ripe almost to a mush.

23   What does this planet need?

24   Just to get a moment in the mind of Gertrude Stein or Einstein, like a tea cup.

25   Can you write in the dark? Can you even think properly, in the dark?

lxxvi

1   I love tying knots, tying furniture to the car roof, tying tomato vines to stakes, etc. There's something about the logical puzzle of a flexible cord and an inflexible object.

2   I love tying things to other things, binding them. And consequently untying, unraveling the knot.

3   After he came up with *Cogito ergo sum*, Descartes started to think about what it is to exist, and what it takes to have an identity. What it is to be a person.

4   The first thing he decided is you have to be singular, not many people but one person. It's a big burden sometimes to only be one thing.

5   When Kathy Acker was in the hospital in Tijuana, she was never alone. I was there every day except the two or three when I drove back to teach. And on those days we paid my brother Valentin to stay with her.

6   Kathy liked my brother. I knew she would. I kind of set it up, a cute guy with a New York accent. I was hoping they'd get a crush on each other.

Then Descartes says you have to persist over 7
time. You can't be you one day and someone else
tomorrow. Or yesterday. You can only be one thing
and that thing has to be the same, all the time.

After a nice bowl of ice cream, Peggy is asleep 8
and having a good dream, sniffing and running
in place.

Most nights I slept in the second bed in the 9
hospital room. I remember the nurse coming in
at night. I woke up when she checked on Kathy,
then fell back asleep.

It was weirdly comforting. 10

Once when I was in London, I went to 11
Sissinghurst with Catherine Lord. It's a garden
built around a medieval tower by Vita Sackville-
West, who had an affair with Virginia Woolf. We
called it Sissyhurst.

One night in the hospital, Kathy and I watched 12
an *X-Files* episode about Agent Scully, who was
dying of brain cancer. They discover that the
cancer was caused by an alien implant and when
they remove it Scully starts to recover.

I asked Kathy if the story was bothering her. She 13
said no, it's just a dumb TV show. But later that
night she woke up with nightmares.

The last thing Descartes says on the subject of 14
being is that you must be discontinuous in space.
You have to have limits. Your body and your
property need to end at a certain point (not too
far either), like at your fingertips. After that is
not-you, or even: someone else.

Someone else is really something to reckon with. 15

16   Everyone in the clinic in Tijuana was dying of cancer. Half were people who believed in alternative medicine, like Kathy, and the other half were those whose conventional doctors told them nothing else could help them. This was their last resort, the last stop before the end.

17   I've always been attracted to figures like Isabelle Eberhardt, Alexandra David-Néel, and Simone Weil. Those women who completely left the world they knew to become someone else somewhere else.

18   Whenever I hear the phrase "untying the Gordian knot," I need to look it up. Gordius, king of Gordium, tied an intricate knot and prophesied that whoever undid it would become the ruler of Asia. Men came along and puzzled over it for months. No one solved it until Alexander the Great came along as a youth. He cut through it with a sword.

19   Now, twelve years after Kathy's death, and ten years after my mother's death, they start to merge.

20   Of course, I would never think to use a sword.

21   That's why I will never be king.

22   Hospital rooms are a lot like airports. They suck all the drama out of things. But they also unify them, so one death is much like another.

23   Simone Weil believed that obligations have precedence over rights. For Weil, unless a person understands that they have certain obligations in life, towards themselves and towards society, notions of right will have no value.

24   Catherine and I also went to the Chelsea Flower Show. It was like a soccer match. I didn't know

that people in mass could have as intense reactions to plants as I do. I finally saw a real Meconopsis, a Himalayan Blue Poppy. Huge, electric blue. I almost cried.

For Weil, one obligation supersedes all others: the obligation to respect and love the Other. 25

lxxvii

One of the few things Peggy has been eating with relish has been pita bread. Lately she just picks at them though, and yesterday she left one sitting with holes gouged out of it that made it look like a skull. 1

I've been visiting Kathy's death. 2

You could say the pita bread reflects Peggy's animal intuition that the end is not far. But I think it reflects our desire to see our own face in everything around us. 3

How did Kathy die? 4

She died of heart failure, like many people with cancer. I had been up the whole night with her, and Connie Samaras arrived on the train the next evening. I took a nap in the other bed in the room as Connie sat with Kathy and held her. 5

I have a memory of seeing Spandau Prison on a visit to Berlin as a kid in the seventies. The last big Nazi, Albert Speer, was imprisoned there. No one could visit him and in fact he wasn't allowed to speak to anyone. One man, alone in a giant prison. 6

But I looked it up today and saw that Speer was released from Spandau almost ten years before my visit. 7

8   I had been sleeping a few hours when Connie woke me because the Mexican nurses said Kathy was dying.

9   Connie and I sat beside her on each side of the bed, stroking her face. We told her she could go if she wanted. We told her it was alright to go.

10 What can I say? The War was everywhere in my childhood, though I was born almost two decades later. Albert Speer, so silent and enormous, he was not even there.

11 Kathy did not close her eyes. She looked at us the whole time.

12 Albert Speer, architect of the Nuremberg Rally and the 1936 Olympics.

13 We knew she was dying because her heart monitor was slow and skipping.

14 Among other things, Albert Speer invented the concept of "ruin value." Major buildings should be built to ensure they leave aesthetically pleasing ruins for thousands of years into the future. Hitler embraced the concept with enthusiasm.

15 Once, Connie Samaras and I went to see the huge white radio dishes used for SETI, the Search for Extra-Terrestrial Intelligence. There are 27 of them, set on tracks in three directions. It's called the Very Large Array.

16 This weekend I saw a photograph of Bill Clinton sitting in his living room, with dozens of framed pictures of him with the world's leaders. Beside him on the sofa was the US presidential seal on a needlepoint pillow.

Kathy's last words were, "Up, up!" She wanted us to raise the back of her bed. 17

After she died, we stayed with her for almost an hour until the mortician arrived. 18

Last week, Peggy was into cheeses and cream sauces. This week it seems like only tomato is ok, though there isn't a lot of protein in pasta with marinara sauce. 19

I guess you are not Bill Clinton unless everything in your surroundings echoes who you are back to you. 20

It was like a train to me. People dying is like a train leaving a station. It's still there for a while, and people can jump off or get aboard. Then it's gone. 21

It was metallic too. Death is grey, with bolts and rivets. 22

Everywhere in New Mexico are hints of aliens, atom bombs, missiles, and spacecraft. Maybe it is because for over three hundred years it was part of Spain and not the U.S. 23

Connie and I came back from Tijuana at four in the morning on a train filled with drunken partiers—sailors and what seemed to be prostitutes, screaming at each other. We thought Kathy might have liked that. 24

When I was a kid, we had one of those vacuum bulbs with a spinning thing inside, from a science museum. There were four squares mounted on a pin, each painted white on one side and black on the other. When you put it in the sun, the inside would spin, proving that light is an active form of energy. 25

lxxviii

1   After Kathy died, I went to Banff for a month, in the middle of the winter. Sylvère Lotringer was there at the same time and every day in the mid-morning we took a long walk through the snow to catch what little daylight there was.

2   I made a mistake yesterday. I remembered wrong. It was Rudolf Hess in the Spandau Prison, not Albert Speer.

3   Part of saying goodbye and moving on is that eventually you have to kill the dead. They certainly don't want to go. You don't want it either.

4   David Wright has not been able to find a job for almost nine months.

5   But you must kill them, which is a more direct way, an active way of saying you let them die.

6   I think this is part of the potency of the vampire myth today. We're less and less capable of killing the dead. Not only are the undead unavoidable, but more and more people seek to join them.

7   At the Huntington Gardens there is a glorious path through a long narrow valley of spiny cacti with silver or gold needles. They are backlit by the sun and they shimmer in an extra-planetary way.

8   The sun is behind them in the afternoon, when the majority of visitors are present. Now that is thinking. Not necessarily about plants, but about people.

9   My friend Nikki couldn't bear to kill her mother, and Nikki was paralyzed for years.

Rudolf Hess was there until he died, but if you   10
look him up, you won't understand exactly what
his crime was. He was a symbol.

He served a life sentence, alone for the last twenty   11
years. The guards were not allowed to talk to him.
The prison was torn down after his death, to
prevent it from becoming a Nazi monument.

Peggy has little appetite for anything I make   12
her, but three times this week she's upended the
kitchen garbage. She hasn't rooted through the
trash since she was a puppy.

I'm still a dog, she's saying.   13

Albert Speer. If it weren't for the War, my father   14
would have become an architect. But he was
thrown out of school as a teenager and ended up
in Buenos Aires, a jewelry designer.

Sometimes I see the problem of sexual fantasies as   15
being about unified bodies. Most of my fantasies
are about one part of me there, and another part
elsewhere, and likewise the other person.

After the fifties, the German government started   16
paying reparations to individuals or families
harmed by the War and the Holocaust. They were
called *Wiedergutmachung*: making good again.

Some of my relatives got them. Some did not.   17
My father's older brother applied because he too
was thrown out of school. My father did not. He
argued with his brother about it. We're alive he
said, and others are not.

If it's possible to walk into death with your eyes   18
open, Kathy did.

19   Today, I spoke to a friend who's flush with success and not as happy as you'd expect. People were happier to commiserate with her failures than to celebrate her successes.

20   Failure is open, everyone is invited to be kind. Success looks hard and cold to those who perceive they are outside it.

21   It's a bit like we treat the living and the dead. People are all too willing to praise the person once the body is cold.

22   Last year, Camille spent a long time deciding if she was emo or goth.

23   This seems to be a very big question for a teenager.

24   I think about eating all the food Peggy won't eat. It's human food, after all. If I could eat it and thereby transfer all the nutrients to her body, I would.

25   And last week, another friend who hates his success. Everyone watches you, he says, and waits for one misstep. All the ones who stood in the way now suck up to you, and all your old supporters can't wait to see you stumble.

lxxix

1   I love the Popeye's chicken at the corner of Hollywood and Cahuenga. I love the food, the people, the decor, and the music.

2   You can tell I'm in a good mood.

3   I've been writing about Dieter Roth's "Literature Sausages," which are made of shredded books mixed with spices and lard and stuffed into sausage casings. Among the authors he chose were Goethe, Günter Grass, Heinrich Böll and Hegel.

I wonder if I have been delivering a few literature   4
sausages myself. Little ones, 25 every few days.
Cocktail literature sausages.

The list is a bastard form, meant to compart-   5
mentalize the wildness of things.

The list is the instrumentalization of language.   6

I remember wanting to drink food coloring as a   7
kid. I wanted to be really green.

There is nothing like lemon zest.   8

For quite a while, there I was feeling like a random   9
thing generator. And what is random about that?

Even enslaved to something as light as the   10
random, you're still a slave.

When my parents got a new TV in the 80s, the   11
man from the store called my mother and told
her she had forgotten the remote control. She
told him they probably didn't need it, but he
insisted she come back for it anyway. Later, she
said to me that she thought remote controls just
were for lazy people.

Draining the battery is good for the phone, right?   12
Or the MacBook? It's like a muscle. Use it or lose it.

Once he got used to the remote control, my   13
father said the second best switch was the Mute
button, but the best one was Off.

For a while Peggy was into pita bread but now   14
she only likes the Russian rye bread from the
Armenian market.

A typical Facebook moment is when you find   15
people you knew from long ago. After high school

you always wondered what happened to them and you're happy to see them. They befriend you, but then they ignore you as they always did.

16   You realize they were never really nice to you, but like a dog you're happy to see them again. And you're still hurt that they don't like you.

17   I am more and more like my parents in my sensitivity to noise. Also to dark restaurants where you can't read the menu. What's up with that?

18   Do you remember those ads for plastic surgery that said, "Why pay all that money for clothes when it's *you* they notice?"

19   I am so tired of making lists I could cry. I'm tired of trying to get people's attention. I just want to shut up and go to sleep.

20   On some days I cannot finish my list because nothing comes. The problem is not with things. The problem is me.

21   If you analyzed the gaps, you would find that I stop when life is too much for me, when things don't come to me, or sometimes when too much comes at once.

22   My father and I used to make fun of my mother's habit of buying side tables. No chink of wall was left open. She had a horror of the vacuum.

23   David Wright said that Peggy was smelling doggy the other day. I can't smell it at all. She either doesn't smell or just smells familiar to me.

24   One of my distinctive "German" memories is once when my brother and I moved the refrigerator so my mother could clean behind it. I

remember all of us cheering as every last speck of dirt disappeared up the vacuum.

Actually I don't think I'd mind if Peggy smelled even doggier.   25

lxxx

After Kathy died, I gave one of her silver skull   1
rings to Danny Babcock. He just called to tell
me it was stolen. But I wonder if Kathy would
have minded the idea of her rings going out in the
world, off on new pirate adventures.

When I was in high school, I loved the corny   2
last line of Edna St. Vincent Millay's poem on
Beethoven: "Music my rampart, and my only
one."

I often measure the success of my day by how   3
much food I've gotten Peggy to eat.

On Monday, I spent the day with the vodka makers   4
at Tru. They are helping me infuse fruit from local
neighborhoods in vodka: Neighborhood Infusions.
There's something about workspaces, a kind of
clarity and purposefulness. It made me happy.

A friend, a philosophy professor, once tried to   5
explain Kant's concept of purposity to me. I never
got it.

Four years ago, I went to the Pope's Palace   6
in Avignon. It's magnificent. What splendor,
considering it was the 13th century. The pope
slept two stories above the treasury where all the
gold was kept. It was a straight line from the gold
to the pope to god.

And that bridge, in Avignon—yes I danced on it.   7

8   Does anyone remember the "Don't hate me because I'm beautiful" shampoo commercial?

9   I was in Home Depot the other day and they were playing "Lola" by the Kinks. Lola's a hot girl who's really a boy. There was something perfect about it.

10   Feed a Child With Just a Click (a Facebook ad).

11   Another time years ago I was walking in Home Depot and this man with a tool belt ran up behind me to say how much he liked my t-shirt. It was one they gave away when the Armani store opened; it had a big nut & bolt on the back and I'm sure it meant something different to him than it did to me.

12   I think they sent you a nut & bolt in the mail and you got a free t-shirt if you brought it into the store.

13   It's like Peggy and I are on a dark road. It's not really sinister, just dark, and you don't know where you're going. You know death is at the end, but just not where the end comes.

14   "Remarks are not literature." Gertrude Stein.

15   LOL

16   Lately Peggy wants to be petted a lot. The dog books say petting is the echo of a lick; it's like her mother licking her as a puppy. It's an affirmation, a reminder that all the parts of her body make up one body, that she's one dog, and that she's here, with me.

17   One reason I feel like I grew up in another century is that in my early years I mostly heard classical music. And I often heard it live, especially from

my uncle George, who was a pianist. My earliest musical memory is probably Schumann, or Beethoven's "Für Elise."

So I learned that music comes from instruments, not radios or stereos. Not really from instruments either, but from people. Music comes from people. 18

David Burns lost his adjunct classes at UC Irvine and hasn't had a paycheck in three months. 19

My uncle George began to lose his memory when I was about eleven. He was some twenty years older than my aunt, Amanda. A few times we found him in our garden, gazing at the flowers. 20

George came to visit my mother, but that was not a good thing. My aunt, my father's sister, couldn't bear that George ended up in my mother's flowers. 21

Once I came home with my cousin Bettina and George wouldn't unlock the door because he didn't recognize us. Bettina started to kick at the door. Her shoes left black scuff marks. They looked like angry brush strokes. 22

Later, when George was in a nursing home, I remember seeing notes between my cousin and my aunt, A to B, and B to A. 23

At another time, I noticed that my aunt Ali, in Buenos Aires, left notes for Martín, a friend of my other cousin, who lived with her for a while. It was the same, A to M, M to A. 24

To me those letters, like math, like algebra almost, seemed warm and intimate. Secretive rather than anonymous, unlike the initials in Kafka, like K. 25

lxxxi

1 Today, Peggy fell and rolled down the stairs. She was dazed and I carried her back up. But later she wanted to go for a walk and seemed fine.

2 After writing one list of 25 Random Things About Me Too and seeing how many people were doing lists, I decided I would do 25 lists of 25.

3 I'm struck by how Peggy can be so diminished and yet also be the same dog.

4 Vanessa Place suggested I do 2500 Random Things About Me Too, 100 lists of 25, but I doubted I had enough to say. I told her I wanted to get to 25, and then I'd think about more.

5 Around 23 or 24 I started to feel panicky, as if I actually wouldn't be able to say everything I needed to say.

6 Peggy is a pitiful sight. She has awful sores on her skin, which she's scratching. I thought they were from flea bites but I think now they're probably cancer lesions.

7 It's harder to actually write about it than just to sit with her.

8 When I am alone, writing, it seems like the most unbearable thing.

9 26 to 33 was great. I've been looking back. It really flowed. Then I hit a slump.

10 I picked up through to 50, even though it was hard to keep it up every day while I was traveling in Colombia.

Peggy still likes to go for walks. Everything with   11
a scent attracts her: urine, rotted things, shit. She
wastes no time on frivolities.

After my mother died I often thought of the Nick   12
Cave song, "Death is Not the End." It isn't the
end. My mother rattles around in my head even
more than when she was alive.

Peggy and I often catch each other's eyes and look   13
at each other. It seems to have a message, but
maybe it doesn't.

I think all it means is affirmation. It means you   14
are here and I am too.

When I was a kid, I remember my aunt Amanda   15
saying, "Let's get down to the real nitty-gritty."

After 53, I hit a big slump. I'm not sure it was   16
because I had too much to say or too little. I
stopped for more than a week. Since then, I
mostly manage two or three days in a row, then I
skip a day. Or more. A week, or ten days.

I was always envious of my friends' parents. Mine   17
seemed so much older. I was afraid people would
think they were my grandparents.

When I hit the low 60's, I again had trouble   18
listing 25.

Now as I work on them, I think ahead, and back,   19
more than I did at first.

I often hear the baby next door crying. I like it.   20
It occurs to me that for millennia it was more
normal to hear babies crying than not.

Many years ago, Hilda, a family friend, took me   21
to meet a famous pacifist, George Moore. He

was very old, a conscientious objector in the First World War. He'd been in jail for seven years for refusing to serve and then he wrote a book about it. Hilda knew him from the prison abolition movement, of which they were both members.

22   We were sitting outside and a fly kept landing on his knee. It was so distracting, I couldn't stay in the conversation. If he was a pacifist, would he just shoo the fly away?

23   Finally he noticed the fly and killed it in one swat.

24   Peggy has big raw patches of skin without hair. It sounds horrible as I write it, but I've already gotten used to it. At first it horrified me.

25   I'm going to finish these lists. It's just hard now when the only "random" thing happening to me is Peggy's steady decline.

lxxxii

1   On the afternoon Michael Jackson died, I was driving from Hollywood to Santa Monica right past UCLA. I didn't know what happened but there was a strange energy, a kind of radioactive cloud.

2   There's a coyote on the hill above my house.

3   As a kid, I learned about California from a Burpee seed catalog. I was looking at a page of petunias and one kind was called Santa Barbara petunias. There was a photo of them in the sun, white, pink and purple. So that was California, flowers in the sun at the end of a block, on a hill over the ocean.

4   Oh, California.

In grammar school we got hearing tests every 5
year. You put a little earpiece by your head and
raised your hand if you heard a high pitched tone.

The earpiece smelled like the alcohol they used 6
to clean it between kids. I remember the smell as
much as the sound.

Remembering is like a photo album, only one 7
that is not organized. A box of photos, some with
names and some without.

Peggy is pretty deaf and it feels harder to 8
communicate, harder to read her. She's different.
I can't tell if she is suffering at all. I feel like she
doesn't much understand me anymore either.

To her, it must not seem like she hears less, but 9
that the world has gotten quieter.

When I was a teenager, I had Joni Mitchell's *Blue* 10
album. Her song about California on *Blue* is
scratchy and tinny but you never forget it after
you've heard it a few times.

As Peggy gets more brittle, there is a bigger 11
difference between us. I'm more human and she's
more animal.

I have Wanda Coleman's fingernail on my 12
bookshelf. It broke off when she slammed her
book on the table at a reading. She stormed out
and I found the fingernail on the stage later.

Kumquats are not like any other fruit. The skin is 13
sweet but the inside is sour. They're kind of zippy.

My psychoanalyst's office was near an old-style 14
barbershop. Once a week, I noticed a big black limo
and a few guards standing around. Then I finally
saw the old man in the car was Ronald Reagan.

15   I accused my doctor of seeing Ronald Reagan without telling me, and she laughed. He came every week to get his hair cut at the barbershop. We talked about my fantasy of her cheating on me with an the ex-president.

16   This week I drove past the house on 26th street where Bertolt Brecht and his wife lived in the 1940s when he was in exile in Los Angeles.

17   What a criminal, Ronald Reagan.

18   My neighbor two houses down has two small security cameras facing up and down the street, and the monitors for the cameras are on his upstairs patio. You can see yourself come and go while walking your dog.

19   I had a coin collection once. I think of that time as one of the most boring periods of my childhood.

20   My mother took me sometimes to a button store run by two old ladies. All the buttons were mixed up in big baskets but they also had old coins so I would get to go through them and buy some instead of buttons. The ladies must have sold anything that was old, small, and round.

21   I remember when I was 20, in France going to pick Lilies of the Valley with my French cousins in the woods.

22   *The Twilight Zone* episode that scared me the most was the one with a kid on an airplane. He sees a monster outside on the wing, but no one believes him. When he looks out the window the monster stares at him, but when the adults look, they see nothing.

23   Maybe the family was emigrating from one country to another.

My mother had a big box of buttons but it was not a button collection or anything like a coin collection. She loved those buttons.   24

In the museum on Ellis Island, there are displays of people's luggage, their letters, quotes from people who came through when they entered the United States. A mother from Latvia, around the turn of the century, said that seeing her daughter immigrate to America was like seeing her into her coffin.   25

lxxxiii

I love sharp knives. Hardly a day goes by without me sharpening a knife.   1

For me, the knife is like the hammer for Nietzsche, his great symbol for philosophy.   2

Today, I just spent time with Peggy but didn't think about any of it.   3

You hear a piano tinkling in the distance. What does it mean?   4

Pay attention.   5

The body without organs: I never really understood what that meant until I saw it in Peggy. She is "populated only by intensities."   6

Peggy does not think about her skin sores, or her cancer. She just moves along. Or sleeps.   7

No organ is constant (Deleuze). Sex organs sprout anywhere. Peggy has orgasms through her nose.   8

There was once an opera singer who lived up the hill from me. I'd hear her practicing with her piano. Where did she go?   9

10   I'm going away for a month and David Wright is staying in my house with Peggy.

11   How can I leave a dying dog?

12   There's that scene at the end of *Titanic* when you see all the photographs above the bed of the old woman who survived the sinking. You see her on a horse, flying an airplane, on an elephant in India. She went on, it says, she decided to live.

13   Certain men only become handsome with time. Look at those early pictures of George Clooney, when he was young and just pretty.

14   Me, the keyboard, grasping for a random thing—all of it can be seen geometrically.

15   Picking lilies of the valley in France seems to be some kind of tradition, maybe an old one. They're called *muguets* and they're native to France, though not to the New World. They're little and grow close to the ground, easier to find if you have a good nose. People fan out to pick them and when they find them they say, "*J'ai trouvé des muguets!*"

16   John Cage had a lifelong interest in mushrooms, and he was a co-founder of the NY Mycological Society. He would take people on field trips to find mushrooms.

17   I'm increasingly forgetful, sometimes fatally. I remember important meetings three hours after I'm supposed to be there.

18   There's a kind of terror in your own mind.

19   I wonder who my neighbors are.

20   John Cage's *Indeterminacy* is a collection of anecdotes or short tales taken from life or books

he read. He used them for readings, flipping randomly from one to another. Each one was supposed to take one minute to read, so the short ones were read slowly and the long ones very fast.

One of my neighbors is a man who I had sex with more than ten years ago when he lived somewhere else. He doesn't remember me but I figured it out from a photo I found on my computer. He's posed there beside the same exotic car he has now.   21

I see him outside his house sometimes and I can tell he does not remember me and I have no desire to remind him.   22

The sun in the pine needles quivering in the wind. What else is more important?   23

Dead rat on my patio.   24

When I lived at the beach, it was grey in the mornings and from the window above the kitchen sink I'd watch surfers in black wetsuits sitting on the glassy water, waiting for the next big wave.   25

lxxxiv

The fireworks were anemic this year. No one has money to pay for flares and rockets. My first thought when I saw them was that this must be what it looks like to burn money.   1

I no longer delete people from my address book when they die. I haven't done it in years. It feels like I am killing them.   2

We watched the 4th of July from above, from David Burns' parents' house in the mountains over the San Bernardino Valley. There was a nearly full moon overhead that almost upstaged everything. Fireworks are humans' attempt to imitate the stars.   3

4   I saw a fish jump in the lake.

5   We live in a diminished world if the only choice
     is to either endlessly rebel against our parents or
     become just like them.

6   When David Burns and I shared a house in the
     mountains, I once found a big hairy tarantula
     crossing the street. I'd never seen one before so
     I caught it in a yogurt container to show people.
     But I left the container on a table in the sun and
     the next day the spider was dead, so I put it into
     the freezer to preserve it.

7   I set the tarantula in a kind of attack pose and left
     it there to freeze dry. When visitors opened the
     freezer, they either shrieked or laughed.

8   When I was a kid, maybe in the Cub Scouts,
     I made a Christmas tree out of an old *Reader's
     Digest*. All the pages got folded into triangles and
     the ends glued together so it made a cone. Then
     we spray-painted them gold, so they didn't look
     like old magazines.

9   Hamburger Helper, Shake 'n Bake, and Rice-a-
     Roni.

10   I made my mother take me to the Cub Scouts
     because it seemed like the right thing to do. My
     brother came too, and my mother was even a den
     mother for awhile. Eventually we all got bored of
     it, but not before I came in second place in the
     balsa wood race car derby.

11   My race car was painted yellow with a brown
     underside and carved to look like a banana. My
     father gave me graphite for the wheels.

12   Another time in different mountains, I found a
     dead bluebird and froze it until I could pluck the

blue feathers and mount them in a frame. But the frozen bird disappeared somehow and I still wonder who threw it out.

Today two guys rang the doorbell to ask if they could wash the sidewalk and pull the weeds for $40 to pay their electric bill.   13

Up the road from David's parents' house is a big Tudor cottage with a plaque that says Shirley Temple House, 1931.   14

The neighbors gave us their old *Reader's Digests* and I was the only one who read them. My mother liked the *New Yorker* but the articles were so long. I remember thinking why read a whole book when you can read ten condensed ones in the same amount of time?   15

Neither of my Davids, Wright or Burns, has a job or the prospect of one.   16

"I often find that having an idea in my head prevents me from doing something else. Working is therefore a way of getting rid of an idea." – Jasper Johns.   17

All those books digested for you without chewing.   18

On TV they're interviewing the US Airways pilot who landed his broken jet in the Hudson River. New Yorkers love this kind of story because it assures them that New York is the exception to all things, and that they are still living in the center of the universe.   19

After Kathy died, I went to a residency in Banff for a month. There are hot springs above the town and I hiked up alone to sit in the hot water in the snow. When I was done I decided to come straight down the mountain under the electric   20 lines rather than walk along the icy road with recklessly speeding cars.

21   The snow was high, so you sort of waddled or rolled down the hill. It was 40 below zero and much further than it looked. I was so tired, I wanted to curl up and take a nap in a snowdrift.

22   It was like a novel in which the main character's friend dies in a Tijuana cancer clinic and a week later he freezes to death in the Canadian Rockies for no reason anyone can think of.

23   In 2006, I saw Patti Smith play an acoustic set at Beyond Baroque. I sat on the floor about 6 feet from her.

24   "I haven't fucked much with the past, but I've fucked plenty with the future."

25   Imagine, though, your plane crash-lands on a river and you survive!

lxxxv

1   Every morning in Banff, Sylvère and I took a different walk in the snow. There was light from 9 to 3 but it felt like the North Pole.

2   A man by the cheese in Trader Joe's told me the New Zealand Grass-Fed Cheddar ($4.99) was really good.

3   He was right.

4   There's a photograph almost ten years later of David Burns, Sylvère and me on kayaks in the Hudson River in upstate NY. Chris Kraus took it. The three of us are in red, yellow and green kayaks and we look kind of like a sporty American family.

When I was a kid, a hippy on the street asked me 5
about the war in Vietnam. Was I pro or con? I knew
what he was asking but I didn't know what pro or
con meant. I figured con was "with," like *café con
leche* or concubine, so I said pro, like prohibit.

Then he lectured me about being a conformist. 6

David Wright's favorite color is red. 7

There are certain questions where you know 8
exactly what the answer is supposed to be. Even if
it's your answer anyway, it's like a trap.

Sylvère was the only person who came from 9
outside San Francisco to visit Kathy Acker in the
hospital there. He was there when she wrote her
will, and he was one of the witnesses.

I remember both of them beaming at me. It 10
brought up a fantasy I had in college, when I first
read Sylvère's name in one of Kathy's books and
figured out that they were lovers. What would it
be like to be their kid, I wondered.

My favorite color is yellow. Or orange. 11

Sylvère flew from NY again to see Kathy about 12
a week before she died in Tijuana. She couldn't
talk much.

My impulse was always to leave them alone the 13
few times I was with them. I think Sylvère would
have liked it, but Kathy asked me to stay. She
didn't know what to talk about.

Is there a better queer piece of art than Robert 14
Rauschenberg's *Bed*?

No one seems to be getting very angry about not 15
having a job, or losing their house, etc. Maybe
that's really why it is called a depression.

16   About twenty years ago, I was driving from the city to our house in the country with my mother on the 4th of July. We were trapped near the bridge in Staten Island by a weird local parade, ordinary people with flags or banners dressed as Frankenstein and Heidi, space robots and Mickey Mouse. There was a school band in shabby uniforms. Some people just wore old hats, or threw a sheet over their heads.

17   We were trapped in traffic and my mother started talking about the War. She and her grandmother had been bombed out of one apartment after another. By the end of the War they had been evacuated to a farm in Poland or what they then called East Prussia. When the Russian soldiers invaded, she said, they were very brutal, and all the women were raped.

18   I realized she was telling me that she and maybe her grandmother had been raped.

19   Peggy is very skinny and determined. From a certain angle she looks like a white arrow. Willpower alone seems to keep her alive.

20   When I was getting my Ph.D., I believed post-structuralist theory, or French theory, as they call it now, was everything. It was not the truth but the key, the method for seeing how the truth was folded or braided with untruth.

21   All this was slowly undone by my experience with my colleague Sande Cohen. In him I saw critical theory used to manipulate, conceal, and intimidate.

22   A white arrow of a dog.

23   When I was a child, I noticed how my mother trembled when she heard sirens, or exploding firecrackers in the distance.

I would not be telling you this if my mother was still alive. 24

My yankee doodle sweetheart. 25

lxxxvi

During the War my mother's aunt, Sonja, worked in a gas mask factory. It kept food in their mouths. By 1943 she was pricking little holes in the masks. My mother said she wasn't so much against the war as she was tired of it. She wanted to go on dates again. 1

If you're driving up the I-5 today, you'll see truckloads of the most beautiful tomatoes. 2

Cantaloupes! 3

While Kathy was dying, I met Chris Kraus for lunch a block from the hospital. She always came down to Tijuana for dental work, where it's cheaper. 4

Chris never saw Kathy in the hospital, because they didn't get along. But we talked about Kathy. Chris admired Kathy more than any living writer. She cared about Kathy even though Kathy didn't care about her. 5

Whenever I drive this way I see trucks carrying new cars, but not this time. 6

You never see those aluminum milk trucks anymore. Or the ones with hazardous liquids. Does it all go in pipes now? Or are they cloaked, driving in secret at night? 7

It could be there is a secret underground highway system. 8

9   During the War my mother stayed for a few nights with one of her school friends outside Köln. The second night was the worst firebombing of the war, and the entire neighborhood she lived in with her grandmother and aunt was destroyed. The friend's family was going to move to the country and they insisted my mother come with them. It was impossible that my mother's family had survived.

10 My mother turned them down. She had to know if her grandmother and aunt were dead. Then she would go on.

11 She found them at a shelter.

12 Wrecked cars, flattened like pancakes and piled into flatbed trucks.

13 David Burns got his unemployment approved.

14 Another truck of wrecked cars.

15 I just passed the gas station where we stopped with Kathy so she could pee on the way to Tijuana. She was so weak we had to lower her out of the back of the van. She pulled up her hospital gown and peed in the sunshine, and she said, "Oh, the sun feels so good on my pussy!"

16 It's at Exit 391, if you want to visit.

17 In the middle of the night, if I met my mother walking to the bathroom or in the kitchen eating something, I couldn't talk to her because it would wake her up. At that point, she was like a ghost in a fairy tale, a figure of enchantment.

18 Halfway between LA and San Francisco there is a sort of cow hell. Thousands of cows on black shit-covered rolling hills waiting to be butchered. You can smell it before you see it.

I used to imagine staging a version of Dante's *Inferno* there, with cows as all the actors.

19

Cara Baldwin calls it Cowschwitz.

20

I'm not suffering as much being away from Peggy as I thought I would. Maybe because I worried so much, I paid in advance.

21

When I was a kid, I found the neighborhood pervert, Frank Cirincione, hiding in the corner of an undeveloped lot we played in. He had his penis dangling outside his pants and he tried to get me to touch it but I wouldn't. Finally, I agreed to touch it with a stick.

22

He was wearing a pair of white briefs over his head with each eye looking through the leg holes. It made him look like a big insect.

23

Every time I drive into San Francisco over the Bay Bridge, I think of Grace Slick singing, "Don't You Want Somebody to Love?"

24

The first time I drove over the bridge into San Francisco years ago, it was in a convertible with the roof down.

25

lxxxvii

The Headlands Center for the Arts is an old military barracks from 1907. We live in the officer's houses and the soldiers' barracks are our workspaces.

1

An index is less a thing than something pointing to the thing, a clue or hint or measure. But you can also see it as a thing in itself.

2

The soldiers' toilets are still in one big room that everyone uses, men and women both. There are

3

thick steel plates between the stalls that clang when you hit them. It's like sitting in a gong.

4 From my thirties into my forties I was afraid there was a terrible power inside me.

5 At my junior high school graduation, the whole class had to sing the Carpenters' "We've Only Just Begun."

6 There is an index and then there is indexicality, the way a thing points at other things.

7 From the top of the hill here you can see San Francisco, and Alcatraz.

8 There are still gang showers here but they've been closed down. Nothing is individual. It's all about a group identity.

9 X marks the spot. And every x is a chiasmus, a crossing, one line or one dimension crossing another.

10 Someone had brought Kathy a copy of Chris Kraus's *I Love Dick* (which she liked) to Tijuana. But when Dick Hebdige came to visit her by surprise, it was lying on the foot of her bed.

11 I starting chatting avidly with Dick and without breaking eye contact, I casually tossed Kathy's pillow over the book.

12 It's the x-ness, as in exile, or x-ray. Or galaxy. No matter how big or how narrow the crossing, you get through.

13 In graduate school my roommate was a medievalist. His pet peeve was finding other people's foolish commentary in library books. All day I'd hear him across the room erasing all the marginalia.

For a long time, I confused Richard Simmons the exercise guru and Gene Simmons of Kiss, wondering how one mediocre person could have two such contrasting careers. I imagined him as the kind of person who could move ahead through willpower alone. 14

The index is a system to make finding information more easily, but still things get re-arranged. 15

You go to a new place, bring nothing with you. You get a room, a workspace. At a thrift store, you get new clothes. You eat different food, make friends with strangers. Is it a new you, or the same you? 16

I've bitten my nails my whole life and occasionally it was a topic with my psychoanalyst. She believed it was a symbol of my repressed anger, which was also the root of my depression. She never exactly said that but I know she thought it. 17

She did suggest that my nail biting was a way of preventing my terrible destructive power from taking over, as if I was chewing off my claws. 18

Wherever you go you see rabbits that, when lit from behind, have supernaturally glowing ears. 19

The story of Dick and Sande Cohen is that of a good man hurt by a bad one. And Nicole Panter (with her half job) was the projectile Sande curled in his fist to throw at Dick. Contempt in every direction. 20

How Sande must have despised Dick, who with no less intelligence but more taste and intuition, wrote one significant book after another. People noticed Dick without his trying. Sande tried and tried until he found he was really only capable of terror. And then we noticed. 21

22   I'm about an hour away from where Hitchcock shot *The Birds*. And you can feel it.

23   Do something radical: write someone a letter, by hand.

24   In the latrines, you hear everyone, women, kids, old men. It's haunted somehow. Perhaps with soldiers.

25   There are quail everywhere too, with those little feather blots over their head like cross hairs.

lxxxviii

1   The index is also a typographic mark, a fist with a finger pointing in one direction, sometimes called a digit.

2   A short walk from the Headlands is the country's only surviving Nike nuclear missile site. From 1955 to 1974, dozens of missiles were armed with warheads more than three times the power of the bomb in Nagasaki. There were 300 sites around the U.S. like this, our last line of defense.

3   It's rare for me to drive across the Golden Gate Bridge and not think of Mark Finch, who walked out to the mid-point one autumn day in 1994, put down his briefcase and jumped.

4   David Wright says Peggy was sad the first day I was gone and barely ate anything but now she's eating again and wants to go for walks.

5   Anyone standing within a quarter mile of just the missile launch was killed by the noise, their soft tissue smashed into hard tissue and bone like hamburger.

6   Vienna is a gloomy place. I had a bicycle for the three weeks I was there and the only time I loved

the city was late at night when I'd ride along the empty Ringstrasse and watch men cruise each other in a 19th century streetscape.

I had sex with a blond ballet dancer who lived   7
in a hundred-year-old apartment building with a glass elevator. He gave me drugs and I rode home spinning on my bicycle. It's a wonder I didn't crash.

Peggy is still alive. What is wrong with me? Did I   8
unconsciously want to stage her death just for the dramatic arc of my hundred lists?

The word "warhead."   9

I remember going ice skating in junior high   10
school. They always played "More" on the organ and I learned the music by heart without ever hearing the lyrics. For some reason, it was the place all the kids tried to smoke, with packets of cigarettes stolen from their parents.

A mile away are the radar stations whose business   11
was "target acquisition." A net of bases and stations stretched around North America to protect us against the Russians.

At that time, the only way into the Headlands   12
was the five-minute tunnel. It's an ancient single-lane tunnel and at each side you have to wait five minutes for the opposing traffic to come through.

Which is the signifier and which the signified?   13

The cellar of the house in which we are staying   14
here is filled with plastic children's toys. But where is the child?

Which is langue and which is parole?   15

16   No one knew if Mark really jumped off the Golden Gate until his body washed up on a beach six weeks later. His body had to be identified with dental x-rays.

17   The double-axle.

18   Park ranger talking about the missile site: "There's a fine line between historical reminiscence and bovine defecation."

19   No one knows why Mark jumped. He was a tall, handsome, witty, brilliant British man, the director of the San Francisco gay & lesbian film festival. He had the world at his feet.

20   There's a single kid's chair in the middle of the attic.

21   Near the end is the reflex: the knee, the joint parts, and sex.

22   Mark was the first person to take me to the Headlands and we huddled together on a foggy beach. We were boyfriends for a few weeks and then it was over, and three years later he was dead.

23   The problem of all theories of language is the world: time & space, self & others, etc., and all that is left out of both: mood, filter, modality, ghosts, echoes, shadows, and memory, all that confounds the idea of time and space.

24   Not one foreign bomber or nuclear missile has ever crossed American soil.

25   When you loved someone passionately and haven't forgotten it, but can't summon up any of the passion at all.

lxxxix

Here's a lesson from history: always capitalize on
a crisis. If citizens of x bomb your city, use it to
start a war on y.   1

The Headlands Center had an "open house" and   2
hundreds of people came through to look at the
artists' work.

Is it really a house and does it mean the house is   3
closed all other times?

Men touch women's butts more than women   4
touch men's butts. I saw it myself all weekend.

There's nothing like a disaster.   5

People are more easily moved by the suffering of   6
others than by their pleasure.

I've been watching the different ways people look   7
at art. There are gobblers and gazers.

I'm a gobbler. I have the vanity to believe that   8
I can march through a gallery and understand
every thing I see in a second. I am a camera.

Some people don't look at art at all. They sort of   9
inhale it. Or if it enters by their eyes, they feel it
in their nose, their teeth.

People tell me about all the sadness and loss in my   10
lists but I don't see it that way.

There's the joy of a list, just finding the words.   11

When I was a kid we went down to Bohack's   12
supermarket to play with bits of dry ice that fell
off the trucks. That's how they kept things cold
once. What a miracle—colder than ice and it
never melts, just turns into smoke.

13   Some people just pose in front of art. They want to be seen in its company.

14   We live in a culture where death is shunned. I think we believe that ignoring things makes them go away, but silence only makes them ugly.

15   Think of Mark Finch in his terrible, inexplicable dive off the Golden Gate Bridge.

16   How do you get to the point of no emotion but through emotion?

17   Art can be wallpaper.

18   Some people don't look at what's before their eyes. The snoopers. Like the woman in our studio this weekend who clicked on my laptop to read my email. As if what you're not supposed to see is the real thing and the stuff on the wall is just a veil.

19   I didn't talk to David today so I don't know how Peggy is. I'll just think she's fine.

20   There's an intense food consciousness here. All day we check into the kitchen and talk about dinner, then after dinner we discuss what we ate. When Keith, the fabulous chef, has a day off, you can't imagine him having a life. It's as if he goes into suspended animation when he's not cooking for us, as we do, when not eating his food.

21   I always collect rocks when I travel. There are certain ones I am always attracted to. Rocks with holes through the middle, two-tone rocks, ones with a white line through them, rocks that look like states, and especially rocks with faces.

22   In Bolinas, I found a rock that was shouting at me from the sand.

The stork could be the most primitive looking   23
of all birds, like a dinosaur, or a bird from *The
Flintstones*.

I think the native people believed in spirit rocks.   24

Near the Headlands there are these huge concrete   25
gun turrets. I was climbing one when a gay man
who seemed to be cruising started coming down
the steps opposite me. He was wearing some kind
of weird shorts or culottes. As he passed me, it
flipped up in front and I saw his plump little
penis jiggling around.

xc

Foghorns.   1

Walking on two feet is a real marvel. You can   2
multi-task, talk while you walk, eat, even read.

Yes, not a day goes by that I don't think of my   3
mother in one way or another. Often when I
wake up and almost always when I see something
she would have liked, especially a new piece of
the world.

Some people walk on all fours, sometimes for   4
their whole lives—though we can't see it.

It's interesting the variety of people I can be   5
attracted to.

Question: is the universe random or is it ordered?   6
Or: am I random or ordered?

Jason Tougaw's great-grandfather, who was   7
schizophrenic, walked out naked on the Golden
Gate Bridge and tried to direct traffic.

Kali, the Hindu goddess of joyful destruction.   8

9   Looking at the sand, I saw striking patterns in the blotches. Then looking at the trees and then the sky, I saw the same patterns and I realized they were in my eyes, not the sand.

10 Kathy Acker and my mother are related somehow, other than by my being with them when they died. They're from different worlds, but something connects them. I can't put my finger on it but it's probably their sense of play.

11 The wireless internet always fades out in the afternoon. I think it's part of a natural cycle. It's best late at night.

12 After my mother's leg was amputated, she still got around. A prosthetic leg that works, she said, is better than a real one that doesn't.

13 One day she was outside pulling weeds and fell into a flower bed. With her prosthetic leg, she couldn't get up and she knew my father wouldn't hear her calling for help. So she started pulling all the weeds she could reach. Eventually she got twisted around and found a way to pull herself up. Then she just hobbled back into the house.

14 I saw a little mail truck driving around here, so little and white in the landscape. It was strangely moving. The mail keeps coming no matter what.

15 Erik Snyder is one of my former mentees who killed himself on father's day four years ago. He called me two weeks before he died, asking for leads on finding a job. I just found his resume on my hard drive.

16 I was in Europe for the summer and I missed his memorial service and everything. I felt like I failed him in every way.

I'd destroy every conceptual art piece on earth to spend an afternoon with my mother again. 17

Not much is random except the present, and even then. 18

I saw a crooked old woman hunched over a broom, talking to herself as she swept. As I got closer, I saw she had a cell phone pressed between her shoulder and her left ear. 19

Some of my troubles in life come from having been a blond child in a Latin American country. My mother said women would run across lanes of traffic just to touch my hair. I think she liked that. 20

Erik was a psychogeographer. He was a poet of the suburbs, where he grew up, near CalArts. He wrote about parking lots, tennis courts, water sprinklers going off at night and getting him wet. 21

"Oh so young, so goddamn young." –Patti Smith 22

What is this training of young writers and artists to live without finding jobs or having hope? 23

My therapist taught me the term "suicidal ideation." It's not when you are suicidal but when suicide becomes something that occurs to you, one option among others. 24

Ideas are powerful. 25

xci

How sweet almost anyone looks, sleeping under two or three blankets. 1

At the beach, I found two more rocks with faces. 2

3   All these cute fake towns around here, they're like Carmel, or New Hope, or Woodstock, NY. They might have been real once but they aren't any more.

4   You are filled with the anguish of losing love, but the love you believe you lost was only your own invention anyway.

5   Virginia Woolf committed suicide by putting rocks in her pocket and walking into a river.

6   I've been thinking about the potential of being attracted to everyone, especially when you contrast it to the consequences of being attracted to no one.

7   There are wild blackberries everywhere around here, but all the bushes are laced with poison oak.

8   Things a sentence is capable of.

9   "Without you I'm nothing." It's funny, but also dreadful.

10   Animals I saw today: seals, a chipmunk, a tick on my collar, a dead bee on my pants, a live bee in the car, a gray owl, a young doe and a young buck deer with short fuzzy antlers, some mangy crows, a doe with two spotted fawns, extremely close, and a banana slug.

11   Without you I'm not me. I imagine you, and who you are.

12   I nominate you as the principality of my life.

13   All different yous, but you see what happens when the referent is taken away.

14   I remember going to a beach in Nantucket or Cape Cod when I was a kid, driving through sand

and pine bluffs, the fresh air and a certain kind of light, and how it seemed completely exotic.

That beach memory might be even older, from Villa Gesell in Argentina, where all my relatives went in the summer. Sand dunes, tall grass and pine trees. 15

Most changes arise from chaos. Maybe the best ones arise from peace. 16

A friend of Erik Snyder's posted two videos they made together four years before Erik died. In one, Erik talks about his hope to "transcend personhood and become the lens of a camera." He talks about visiting his old high school playing field and wanting to inhabit it like a ghost. 17

When you listen to Erik two things are clear: he thought a lot about the hauntedness of the world, and he did not feel equipped to handle the weight of survival, or work, or meaningless jobs. 18

Villa Gesell was all sand dunes in the 1930s, until my uncle Tim helped tame the sands with grasses and pine trees. 19

Tim was my father's older brother and he later ran an enormous *estancia*, a cattle ranch. He was the first in the family to immigrate to Argentina, a sort of artsy German Jewish cowboy. My father and his sisters always thought he was gay. 20

Everywhere I go, I try to get in the water, even the coldest water, like in New Zealand or Northern California. There's no philosophy behind it. I just jump in. 21

The water is there. You're there, but not for long. The solution is obvious. 22

23 My father and especially my mother always insisted on a person's right to commit suicide, especially an old person. It was a common topic of dinner conversation, like the Holocaust.

24 I'm so tired of this. Why can't I have random things about you?

25 Point Reyes is the windiest and foggiest place on the U.S. coast. It's a good metaphor.

xcii

1 A few years ago, I took care of a friend who was in electroshock therapy. She had been depressed for years, tried everything, and was suicidal. ECT is the treatment of last resort.

2 Since her health insurance covered almost nothing, X had to live at home and three other friends and I coordinated taking care of her.

3 We often hear the foghorn from the lighthouse nearby even when there is no fog, even in the day.

4 It's a good thing poison oak can't just blow on you.

5 One of us drove X to the treatments, left her, and another had to pick her up later then stay with her for four hours in case she had any seizures.

6 We watched bit by bit as X lost her short term memory, then her long term memory, until what remained was what you might call her personality, her core self.

7 We knew this new person better in a way than her earlier, depressed self.

I took a hike behind the house again to the empty 8
gun turrets. You don't really need to go far around
here to cruise for gay men.

If you just stand still, they will come to you. 9

After the end of the treatments, we weren't needed, 10
and I saw X every few days as she became herself.

Eventually all of her came back, all the pieces 11
reassembled, and she wasn't depressed anymore.

The only thing X didn't remember was the six 12
weeks of ECT, the trips to the hospital, and losing
her memory.

I've been singing to myself a lot, humming, 13
whistling. There's so much space around me here.

Foghorns are comforting. A slow heartbeat of 14
some giant whale inside of whom we live.

Getting everyone to think you're smart and then 15
making something really simple is much easier
than people believing you're simple but just
happened to make something smart.

The rocks I had in my pocket the other day 16
scratched the face of my iPhone. I take this as
an indicator that these two technologies are not
compatible.

A great burden in the world is having people 17
think you're smart and believing that every new
thing you do is smarter than the last.

On the radio today, reporting on the moon 18
landing forty years ago, they played the famous
recording which sounded like this: "One small
step for man, crackle, one giant leap for man-
crack-kind."

19   Peggy is doing ok. She's eating again and she goes for walks with David Wright. All she wants is to go on walks. David says she's mostly like she was six weeks ago. Her skin condition was from mites, and new pills are making it better.

20   I almost can't think about Peggy because then I'd leave immediately and drive home fast and crawl into bed with her right away.

21   There's nothing very random about these lists. I edit them though, to seem random.

22   They are randomesque.

23   Every day you learn again that there is only one way to be. You have to be yourself.

24   Is there any kind of art which doesn't require your participation?

25   Even conceptual art, which can just be an idea, but an idea in your head which arrived there via someone else's head—and you let it in.

xciii

1   The only way I've escaped the great anguishes of lost love is to live in the present.

2   I once had sex on the roof of a tall building in New York with a guy I knew from UCLA. I ran into him in a club in NY and went to his house.

3   Actually there was second guy there and we three had sex together. It was a hot day and I remember being naked on the roof and looking out over the city. It was one of those old buildings that narrow toward the top, like the Empire State building.

The guy was from Arkansas and went to UCLA   4
but I can't remember his name. His stepfather
was a car dealer and in LA he had a convertible
Chrysler. We had sex about six times over a few
years. He was sweet.

Last night, I dreamt I was bitten by a snake who   5
clamped down on my arm. I started wringing it by
the neck to get it off, until another snake, a smaller
one, jumped up and bit the snake that bit me.

David Burns identified the big snake as an artist   6
friend, but I think all the snakes are me. I attack
myself, then attack my attacker for attacking me.

I had my iTunes on shuffle and suddenly I heard   7
my ex-boyfriend, Mike Kelly, singing with his
rock band. It was the mid-80s and they played
the Roxy, Madame Wong's, and the Anti-club.

I remember once joking with the girlfriends of the   8
other guys in the band that we were rock wives,
though we didn't get the full ride since the band
never got signed. This came just after the geekiest
time in my life, as a critical theory junky. I guess
in a certain way it saved me from something, but
I don't know what.

There must be some relation between shuffle and   9
randomness.

You know how teenagers say, "you're so random,"   10
meaning erratic, or not reasonable?

There is so much I have not said about the men   11
I've loved.

Sylvère Lotringer once gave me a long article   12
on his interviews with Jacques Latrémolière,
the psychiatrist who administered electroshock
treatments to Antonin Artaud.

13   This was during the War, when Artaud was in an asylum. What better way to deal with the insanity of fascism than to go mad?

14   The other night I dreamt I was driving a big clunky truck and I hit another clunky truck, but the truck felt like my body and the other truck like another sort of big, sticky body.

15   We're staying in a former army base called Fort Barry, and right near us is Fort Baker, and Fort Cronkhite. I wonder if there is a Fort Da, which would be really nice.

16   *Da* and *fort* are the German words for here and gone. Freud picked up on them when he saw a child playing with a ball, tossing it under the sofa and watching it bounce back. It's here—*da*—when it's here but also in some way here (or there) when it's gone.

17   Artaud mostly talked to his psychiatrist about God.

18   Icy water always reminds you of yourself. There's no one else in that cold ocean with you. You're reminded of you through a kind of shock therapy.

19   It seems I can't stop my random things from turning into stories.

20   I once met Leonardo DiCaprio at a Christmas party thrown by a rich entertainment lawyer and social worker. Also Tobey Maguire and Kirsten Dunst. All I can say is that you'd never guess they were special unless you already knew.

21   The social worker and the entertainment lawyer were a gay couple, friends of my boyfriend. We'd often joke that they were paid inversely to the amount of good they actually did in the world.

You're so random.   22

I keep finding feathers here, and they all look like   23
parts of the same bird, as if it shed everything for
me as part of a prolonged message.

Fort-Da is how we learn about the persistence of   24
things despite our witnessing them come and go.

Another way to say this is that we learn about the   25
idea of presence and absence.

xciv

What art would you say is not site-specific?   1

If you see, hear or feel it, if it enters your mind,   2
you are the site.

And are words not a site of their own? Letters, a   3
mouth, the golden gate.

After I finished my master's degree at UCLA in   4
the mid-eighties, I decided America really wasn't
for me. I signed up for an exchange program in
Paris and intended never to come back.

But two months before my departure, I met Mike   5
Kelly, my rock singer boyfriend, and fell in love.

We lived in Manhattan Beach during the years of   6
the McMartin pre-school molestation case, which
unfolded at first in the local paper. Prompted
by untrained police investigators, the children
starting telling stories of sexual abuse, ritual
sacrifice, and satanic worship. It became the most
expensive criminal trial in the United States.

For many years there, you would not dare look   7
at a child on the street. When you saw a group
of kids coming, you crossed to the other side and
looked down at your feet.

8   David Wright says Peggy has stumbled a few times and fallen down the stairs twice. Like the first time it happened, she was very dazed but then wanted to go out for a walk anyway.

9   There are endless trails to hike in the Headlands, but in the end all of them connect. It's sort of a spiral.

10   One thing that militates against randomness is gravity.

11   Headlands = mind space.

12   Gravity has the power to anchor us, to hold us up against the dirt.

13   It's David Wright's birthday today! On this day, x years ago...

14   We like to use x to signal discretion, but also to veil our forgetfulness. Let x = a variable.

15   At the store, I noticed that watermelons have shrunk to the point of being called "personal melons."

16   I feel like I could really sing the Ballad of the Beautiful Davids!

17   It still surprises me when I notice how many of Freud's ideas live in my head. It's as if they were always there.

18   One phrase that really spooks me is "a child is being beaten."

19   Everyone at the Headlands has access to the refrigerator of leftovers from dinner, but the poor (and unpaid) interns often beat out the artists-in-residence for the food.

XCV

A person imagines he hears a child far off   20
somewhere being beaten, and he becomes very
agitated.

Freud says the first reason is because you are   21
secretly glad, and guilty, that your sibling or rival
somewhere is being punished.

Or, masochistically, it is really you who is being   22
beaten, and this reflects both your fear of and
your strange desire for punishment.

Probably if I had moved to Paris after my master's   23
I would have either finished my Ph.D. there or
dropped out, and never come back to America
or academics.

In the third stage, you again feel it is another   24
child being beaten, but this carries an unsettling
erotic charge for you.

I wonder if there is anyone who feels the truth of   25
the world outside as accurately and intensely as
they feel their own truth.

XCV

I've always been attracted to rattlesnakes and   1
scorpions. Whether you think they are symbols
of evil is a question of perspective.

For me, it's their intense concentration, the aura   2
of power.

Peggy has been eating pretty well, though in the   3
last two days she hasn't eaten anything and threw
up twice. But David says her bald patches have
almost grown back, the light parts before the dark
ones.

4   For a long time, I used the email address scrollo@
aol.com, which I took from my ex, Scott Carollo.
People thought scrollo had something to do with
scripts or scrolls or calligraphy.

5   I'd been using Scott's AOL account and then
took it over after we broke up. In retrospect, I
see it like marrying someone in order to have a
new last name. Many women I know have done
this as well. And kept the last name long after the
divorce.

6   It doesn't take a brain surgeon to see that I needed
to hold onto Scott, but I guess I should ask him.
He's a therapist now.

7   On Tennessee Valley Rd in Mill Valley, I noticed
that behind the fruit stand were all these
neglected, unpicked old fruit trees, peaches,
plums and apricots. But the woman at the stand
didn't know anything about them and had never
sold anything from them.

8   That's America, isn't it?

9   There was a wedding here this week and I saw
them taking photographs outside. The bride
looked like a white puff surrounded by black
sticks (the men) in the fields.

10   Neither of my parents ever intended to return to
Germany.

11   Long ago I saw a film, *Deutschland Bleiche Mutter*.
In English it's "Germany, Pale Mother."

12   My mother's father died of tuberculosis and
afterwards her mother abandoned her to remarry.
Her new husband only wanted to take one child,
not two. So her mother gave up the oldest of two
daughters, my mother. She was four years old.

My mother was taken in by her grandmother 13
on her father's side. They were so poor, that
sometimes they moved out in the night when
they owed too much money on rent.

There's nothing like a dandelion seed head in the 14
sun. But if you pick them, you lose them.

Unless of course you first spray the dandelions 15
with hair spray to hold them in place.

When my mother went to visit her mother's new 16
family, she was jealous of their nice house and
the bedrooms of her younger half-sisters. She was
introduced to them as their aunt, not their sister,
because her mother wanted to seem younger than
she was.

We drove through the spooky five-minute tunnel 17
near here and suddenly everyone around us
starting honking, a spontaneous horn chorale.

I would have finished earlier if I didn't keep 18
forgetting random things.

How did Samuel Barber's *Adagio for Strings* get to 19
be the ubiquitous soundtrack for the tragedy of
war, or modernity, or time?

Wandering around the Headlands, you have 20
to wonder if it isn't all laced with underground
tunnels and roads. People say the whole country
might be, and that subway systems like BART
and the LA Metro are really for the military to get
around without being seen by satellites.

A blue jay swoops from the roof above me down to 21
the grass, pulling my eyes from the sky to the earth.

There are so many scowling young men riding 22
bicycles on the hills here. They have a look of

steely determination, as if trapped in a primal struggle between them and the mountain. They glare at the cars as if we are intruding on something sacred.

23   They could just be locked in a struggle with technology, or with themselves.

24   In a few days, I'll be reunited with Peggy.

25   It seems that once bicycles were primarily associated with pleasure.

xcvi

1   A lot of impersonators learn from how others impersonate people, especially celebrities. Essentially, they impersonate impersonators.

2   One last jump in the ocean today, alone and naked, off a rock with my eyes closed.

3   The water is so much brighter than you expect.

4   I once sat two seats from Jean-Paul Gaultier in a theater in Avignon to see a play by Dennis Cooper.

5   Imagine why anyone would want to go over Niagara Falls in a barrel?

6   What would they see?

7   I remember there's one kind of clear quartz you identify by the fact that everything you see through it appears doubled.

8   Consider the intern. The position of the unpaid intern means always waiting for something, always in the background, surrounded by complaints.

There are artists who never leave their Blue Period.   9

My training in life was always to be more analytical. Analyze what you think and then analyze your analysis. Then start another round.   10

Maybe that's why I need to jump into the cold ocean.   11

The Germans have the word *Mischling* for a person of mixed race, like half German and half Jewish, like my father's family.   12

I'm leaving here soon. I wonder what will remain when I'm gone.   13

Does everyone get to have a Blue Period? Certainly not everyone gets to have a Rose Period.   14

I picked some stinging nettles near here and brought them to the chef, who said he wanted to cook something with them, soup or pizza, but he never did.   15

More Picassos have been stolen than the work of any other artist. Lest you take this at face value, remember that he also produced over 50,000 pieces.   16

Stinging nettles are so nasty, but I've always wanted to taste nettle soup.   17

In Germany old people with arthritis whip each other with stinging nettles. Even though it's supposed to be about arthritis, it's hard to imagine it doesn't have something to do with being German.   18

Maybe the sting just distracts you from your arthritis.   19

20   What will happen to all these people without jobs?

21   Someone just came into our studio, which is all packed up for the trip home. A man stuck his head in the door to look around and I said sorry, there's nothing here. He shrugged and smiled. Oh, I said, I'm here, I should say. Yes, said the man, with a French accent. That's the installation.

22   People seldom pay attention to how they feel when they are ok, when things are ok. All our attention goes to our anxiety, longing, or sadness.

23   Tide pools.

24   A message from beyond.

25   A lot of photographers learned to photograph primarily by looking at photos.

xcvii

1   I did not think Peggy could get any thinner, but she has. She's all angles, like a folded lawn chair. She hasn't eaten in three days.

2   *Murder She Wrote* and *Please Don't Eat the Daisies* are the only TV shows about writers that I can remember. And only two professors: *Gilligan's Island* and *Nanny and the Professor*. But I think Mrs. Muir of *The Ghost & Mrs. Muir* was a writer too.

3   It's shocking to be back home in summer weather after all the cool fog last month.

4   The other day I picked blackberries in the sun and ate them while I talked on my cell phone with my father.

I talked to his wife Nina and somehow the   5
blackberries reminded her of Black Mountain
College, where her father taught and she herself
spent a year.

Peggy is sleeping next to my desk, not curled up   6
really, but in a sort of pointy fetal position.

Range plant, a parasite that looks like tangled   7
orange threads, called Dodder.

If ever a plant looked like it was from outer space,   8
it's Dodder.

David Burns' dog Radar ran away last night   9
and I spent an hour today driving around the
neighborhood looking for him.

When you play word games like Scrabble, what   10
you really learn are only Scrabble words.

Radar got his name because he was a stray dog   11
who appeared one day at David's house—a skinny
black mutt—just as David predicted he would.

Next to the house where we stayed last month is   12
an adjoining mirror house, equal and opposite to
our own.

They were originally officer's houses, and Vanessa   13
Place told me that the officers were evaluated not
just on their performance but on their family's
appearance and behavior. Often a teenage girl
would disappear for six months and return
looking thinner, probably after having had a baby.

Everyone who gets Headlands residency is later   14
considered an alumnus, and can come back for
two weeks every year. A perpetual residency.

The only familiar way I can connect to Peggy is by   15
sleeping next to her.

16   It's a silent duet.

17   San Francisco has the advantage of countless hills, bays, and view points: endless vistas from which it can look at itself.

18   You can't really see Los Angeles.

19   I don't think it's time to put Peggy to sleep yet. She's almost a ghost, but still more present than absent.

20   The one good quality about a chat window is you can just close it, or ignore it, in a way you can't really do with another person in the room.

21   When you close a real window, it's still there, waiting.

22   It's easier to do something if someone is paying attention.

23   I suppose that's a problem, but so what?

24   Last week I took a walk in Mill Valley through their dog park, where I overheard people talking about competing in the "Cutest Dog in Mill Valley" contest.

25   I wish we could talk about you instead of me.

xcviii

1   My ears hurt. In the past, I was guilty of abusing my ears with q-tips and since then, I am very cautious with them.

2   Sometimes I can't believe what I'm hearing.

3   A doctor once told me that there's an ecology in there that you can disrupt by cleaning your ears

too often, especially with witch hazel or hydrogen peroxide.

I remember being obsessed with Strauss' waltz, "On The Beautiful Blue Danube." It must have been after I saw *2001: A Space Odyssey*, but I also remember that it was the call signal of a television station in Germany that I watched all the time on a visit when I was twelve.   4

It's about that "tin tin, tun tun," like quotation marks.   5

Or what precedes it, the "da da da," which is like a question.   6

Da da da, tin tin, tun tun.   7

The question gets repeated, quoted, asked again and again. It builds tension.   8

And then comes the answer: everything. Or the answer is modernity, or here, or now.   9

Here we are.   10

Peggy hasn't eaten in almost a week, but she still wants to go for walks.   11

Everyone says you'll know when it's time to put your dog to sleep, and since I feel like I don't know, it isn't time yet.   12

Garbage pickers all over the world are in trouble. The prices for recyclable paper, glass, metal, and plastic have fallen by 80%. There's more things to recycle and too many people trying to do it.   13

"The Beautiful Blue Danube" is feather-duster music. It's good for cleaning. I can see the video. Clean it like this, like that, sweep it like this, like that, polish like this, etc.   14

15   It's that French horn, wise and woodsy, hunting or heralding.

16   You get caught in the whirlwind without realizing that the whirlwind is one generated by your listening.

17   I took a walk last night with Peggy. I heard babies crying, televisions, a man on a telephone telling someone else, "It's not your fault." It's a full moon on a summer night and they're shooting a film on the deck of a house on the hill above me. The house is lit with reflectors, people are fussing, and the city skyline is in the distance.

18   Yesterday I read about "spagoers" in *The New York Times*. They are not people who eat at Spago but those who go to spas.

19   Life is moving very fast.

20   "The Beautiful Blue Danube" must be a bon bon, a great conductor's piece.

21   It's one of those things I thought was art but then I learned was kitsch. Like Broadway musicals or Impressionism.

22   I feel like my list should conclude with Peggy's death. It would give the sense of an ending, a narrative resolution.

23   My car was covered in stains from the eucalyptus trees so I washed it. Now it seems to not only look bigger, but also drive better.

24   When Jack Kerouac wrote "no time for poetry but exactly what is" I think he meant that poetry was useless compared to experience.

25   There isn't too much beauty in the world.

xcix

I always wanted a friend named Eileen because 1
then I could say Hi I.

Peggy has new habits, even now. Suddenly she 2
likes to be picked up and she sort of snuggles into
my arms.

Finally, I understand that Peggy is not one dog. 3

I wonder if I would have done better in the era 4
of letters of introduction rather than the era of
googling people.

And calling cards, and little card holders in the 5
foyer.

A valediction is a farewell, like at the end of a 6
letter.

My favorite closing in French letters goes like this: 7
*Veuillez agréer, Madame ou Monsieur, l'expression
de mes sentiments les plus distingués.* "Please
receive, Madam or Sir, the expression of my most
distinguished sentiments."

Radar, David Burns's dog, ran away a week ago 8
and is still missing.

Yesterday, David Wright called the vet for me and 9
we made an appointment for tomorrow at 1pm
to have Peggy put to sleep.

For the French, it is traditionally not considered 10
appropriate to begin a paragraph with the first
person singular *je* in a letter.

After I'm done, will there be a cloud of me? 11

Perhaps all of us have an appointment with death, 12
but we know when Peggy's is, and not Radar's.

13   There are words you can't translate from German, like *doch*, *mal*, and *eben*. They are modal particles, which means they don't alter the meaning of a sentence but they add emphasis. They are really like stress marks.

14   Radar went from being a stray to becoming a stray. Another way to say it is that his radar did and didn't work.

15   If I could only press my forehead to the trackpad and have you see what I mean.

16   Instead I'm pressing my fingers to the keyboard.

17   How would the world be different if we were paid and praised to be googling, smoking cigarettes, and eating junk food?

18   When my mother was dying, I pressed my forehead against hers. She was in a coma. I think she knew what I meant, though.

19   Suddenly there was one mind. Everything was calm, and there was no more distinction between dead and alive, here or there. Everything was gone and everything was there at the same time. There were no opposites.

20   Yesterday, we went to the beach in Venice and I swam alone, but there was too much loose seaweed around me so I came back out.

21   David saw four dolphins playing right behind me, but I didn't see them at all.

22   The one thing I feel confident in saying is that making these lists has given me a sense of my own specificity.

23   My bed is a desk. I sit here writing. You know

those notes that have "from the desk of" printed on top of them? They should really say "from the bed of."

I wonder if we can communicate with other species.   24

I can and cannot communicate with Peggy, but like I said, I'm not sure if she is another species.   25

c

There's a difference between narrative and association. One is not natural.   1

I met Lotte Lenya once when I was a teenager. My aunt knew her through the Goethe Institute in NY. We all went for lunch together at Horn & Hardart, Lenya's favorite place to eat. It was the first and I think the last automat, where you pick your warm food through little glass doors in a wall.   2

I like the words preternatural, pellucid, and limpid, and the phrase gin clear. Words with the same wildness hidden inside them as gin. It's a known fact that the worst drunks drink gin.   3

In the hospital one night, Kathy woke up and asked me for the list. When I asked her what list, she said the list to call the animals, to call them back home.   4

The New York Times says that as the economy worsens, there are more laws against begging, loitering, or sleeping on the sidewalk.   5

If you look in a mirror, you think you see you but you see a reflection of you, you as you may appear to others. But thinking that it's you can be a fascinating error.   6

c

7   Lenya disapproved of me not eating all my food. She glared at my almost full bowl of borscht.

8   You see, she said with her accent, the eyes are bigger than the mouse.

9   We're leaving in a minute to take Peggy to the vet to be put to sleep.

10   The truth was I didn't really like the borscht and had only picked it because it was pink.

11   I'm thinking of the "aesthetics of administration," in which you set up a paradigm or hypothesis, a set of conditions, and then you follow them through systematically.

12   Other people inhabit us all the time.

13   My mother entered my head through my forehead. I invited her in. Kathy too. Eventually all the dead people I know will live inside me. And then I will go live inside someone else.

14   Near the end of *Blade Runner*, the last replicant is dying and says to Harrison Ford, "If you could only see what I've seen."

15   Anyone can sing out of tune, but it takes brilliance to make it great without falling into tune.

16   I'm not young anymore, but I feel like I am. Everything inside is worn shiny and smooth.

17   In 1963, Lenya got a part as the communist agent in the James Bond movie *From Russia With Love*. In the final scene in the film, she wore a pair of shoes with mechanized knives so she could stomp people to death. Later in interviews, she said that when she met new people, the first thing they looked at was her feet.

c

I remember *The Russians are Coming!* 18

Obviously, in the act of gleaning, what you 19
primarily find is what is cast off. No one casts off
something they want.

If someone grew the golden peaches of 20
Samarkand, there would be an armed guard in
front of their house, but the bitter oranges rot on
their sidewalk.

And in tossing us hateful comments, people are 21
giving out something they themselves do not
value, their own bitterness.

Dear God: remember that Peggy is a cat and a 22
dog, a person and an alien all wrapped in one.

As you get older, you start to see forgetting is as 23
important as remembering.

It's good to forget. 24

Two years ago, I sat with my 95-year-old aunt in 25
the hospital. She was very sick, and delirious. She
told us something was missing. First we thought
she said *Schwein*, pig, a missing pig, but then she
said no, *Stein*, the stone, where was the stone? She
told us she wanted the stone, but we told her it
was already there, under the table, and that was
enough for her. Then she stopped asking for it.

Matias Viegener is an artist, author and critic who teaches at CalArts. He is one of the members of the art collective Fallen Fruit, which has exhibited internationally in Mexico, Colombia, Denmark, Austria (Ars Electronica), LACMA, the Yerba Buena Center for the Arts, and ARCO 2010 in Madrid. He writes regularly on art for *X-tra* and *ArtUS*, has recently published in *Cabinet, Journal of Aesthetics & Protest, Radical History Review,* and *Black Clock,* and is the co-editor of *Séance in Experimental Writing* and *The Noulipian Analects.*

Kevin Killian is a San Francisco-based poet, playwright, novelist, and critic. His books include *Bedrooms Have Windows, Shy, Little Men, Arctic Summer, Argento Series, I Cry Like a Baby, Impossible Princess, Action Kylie,* and two volumes of *Selected Amazon Reviews.* Kevin Killian's new novel is called *Spreadeagle,* from Publication Studio.

ACKNOWLEDGEMENTS

Thanks to Amanda Ackerman, Diana Arterian, Christopher Hershey-Van Horn, Courtney Johnson, Nikki Halpern, Coco Owen, Vanessa Place, Christine Wertheim, David Wright, and especially Teresa Carmody.

Thanks also to my many interlocutors, visible and invisible, who read and often commented upon my text as it unfolded over time. Their presence indisputably altered its outcome.

A portion of this book was published in *The &Now Awards: The Best Innovative Writing,* Robert Archambeau, Davis Schneiderman, & Steve Tomasula, eds. Lake Forest, IL: Lake Forest College Press, 2009.

ƒ

LES FIGUES PRESS
Post Office Box 7736
Los Angeles, CA 90007
www.lesfigues.com